FC
106
.C5
J56
1992

Humber College
Lakeshore Campus

W9-AEQ-108

0 0 4 3 4 6 1 7 9   3/9

16.2   1068019   1995 01 09

JIN GUO

*Voices of Chinese
Canadian Women*

162136627

HUMBER COLLEGE
LAKESHORE CAMPUS
LEARNING RESOURCE CENTRE
3199 LAKESHORE BLVD WEST
TORONTO, ONTARIO M8V 1K8

DISCARD

The Women's Book Committee

Chinese Canadian National Council

women's
PRESS

The title comes from an ancient Chinese saying
"jin guo is as strong as xu mei." Jin guo literally means
jewellery worn by women. This is a common reference
that women are as brave and as strong as men.

CANADIAN CATALOGUING IN PUBLICATION DATA
Main entry under title:
Jin guo — voices of Chinese Canadian women

ISBN 0-88961-147-5

1. Chinese-Canadian women — History.* 2. Chinese-Canadian women — Social
conditions.* 3. Women immigrants — Canada. 4. Canada — Emigration and
immigration — History. 5. China — Emigration and immigration — History. I.
Chinese Canadian National Council. Women's Book Committee.

FC106.C5J56 1992   305.48'8951071   C92-095053-1
F1035.C5J56 1992

Copyright © 1992 Women's Book Committee, Chinese Canadian National Council

Editor: Momoye Sugiman
Copy editor: Tamai Kobayashi
Cover design: Kok-Kwan Shum
Cover photograph: Henry Haw Collection. Haw Family, Montreal 1905.

All rights reserved. No part of this book may be used or reproduced in any
manner whatsoever without written permission except in the case of brief
quotations embodied in critical articles and reviews. For information address:
Women's Press, Suite 233, 517 College Street, Toronto, Ontario, Canada M6G 4A2.
This book was produced by the collective effort of Women's Press.
Women's Press gratefully acknowledges the financial support of the Canada
Council and the Ontario Arts Council.

Printed and bound in Canada
1 2 3 4 5 1996 1995 1994 1993 1992

Dedicated to
all Chinese Canadian women

HUMBER COLLEGE L. R. C. (LAKESHORE)

Date Due			
MAR 0 7 1995			
MAR 1 7 1995			
MAR 1 7 1995			
OCT 0 7 1997 OCT 1 4 1997			
OCT 2 8 1997			
OCT 2 8 1997			
FEB 2 5 1998			
FEB 1 3 1998			
APR 1 3 1998			
APR 0 9 1998			

HUMBER COLLEGE L.R.C. (LAKESHORE)

CONTENTS

ACKNOWLEDGEMENTS

Many thanks are due to many people for the creation of this book. Without any doubt, the greatest thanks go out to the over 130 women who shared their stories with us, giving us the material and inspiration for this book.

We would also like to thank the countless volunteers who helped out at different stages of the book, such as Joan Huang, Nancy Ing, Kathy Jong, Ming Kit Kwan, Belinda Lee, Joeanni Li, Valerie Mah, Valerie Thoo, and all the friends who helped with translation. Special thanks to Patricia Chew for facilitating the discussion which appears as the epilogue.

This book was made possible through the work of Christina Chu who travelled across Canada to interview all the women, Nancy Li who transcribed and translated most of the Chinese interviews, and May Yee and Terry Woo who were involved as writers, researchers and editorial assistants. Also, thanks to the staff of the CCNC national office for all their help — especially Stella Ng and Shana Wong, and to the CCNC local chapters across Canada for setting up many of the interviews. And special thanks are due to Momoye Sugiman who did the final, substantive editing and restructuring of our manuscript.

We would also like to express our appreciation to the Secretary of State's Multiculturalism Directorate and the Ontario Ministry of Citizenship for the grants which made this book project possible — and to the Multicultural History Society of Ontario for storing our collection of taped interviews and photographs in their archives.

In addition, we are grateful to Paul Yee for his insightful criticisms of our manuscript and to the women at Women's Press in Toronto for all their support and enthusiasm, particularly former managing editor, Maureen FitzGerald, and editor, Angela Robertson.

There are many others to thank, so please forgive any oversights. The writers, editors and editorial committee take full responsibility for any shortcomings in this book.

Editorial Committee
Jin Guo: Voices of Chinese Canadian Women
The Women's Book Committee, CCNC,
Amy Go, Winnie Ng, Dora Nipp, Julia Tao,
Terry Woo and May Yee

INTRODUCTION

Why We Decided to Publish This Book

Canada's Chinese community possesses a long and rich past in this country. However, little of our history has been recorded. Canadian history textbooks have focused on English and French explorers and politicians, ignoring aboriginal peoples, people of other racial and cultural backgrounds, women and workers. The few texts which do mention Chinese Canadians talk primarily about the history of the *men* — the infamous exploitation of Chinese workers who built the Canadian Pacific Railway and the "bachelors" of early Chinatown who were separated from wives and children because of prohibitive immigration laws. The imbalance in the documents can be explained by historical demographics. Chinese men here far outnumbered Chinese women for a long time. However, women's history is equally as important as men's history, regardless of numbers. A few historians, such as Paul Yee and Anthony Chan, have tried to include women's experiences in their books — but in general the stories of Chinese Canadian women have been sadly neglected.

But now out of the silence, emerges *Jin Guo: Voices of Chinese Canadian Women*, an oral history book project of the Women's Issues Committee of the Chinese Canadian National Council. This book is an attempt to fill in some of the gaps. The initial idea was conceived about seven years ago as a booklet. However, it soon evolved into a book because there was so much to say. We interviewed across Canada about 130 women in Chinese and English over a six year period. Some were born in Canada and others immigrated from China, Hong Kong and other parts of the world. They ranged in age from nineteen to eighty-five. The interviewees responded to a set of standard questions. Over three hundred hours of conversations were collected.

Many photographs, some very historically significant, were

collected from the women interviewed. Some of these appear in the photo section in the middle of the book. The other photos in this section are from the Chinese Canadian Women's Photo Exhibit, first shown in 1987 in Toronto.

Because many of the pioneer women were illiterate, they left few writings. Many of their male counterparts were also illiterate, but those who were able to read and write rarely considered the activities of women worth mentioning in their own memoirs. Given the scarcity of material, the CCNC's Women's Book Committee went to the women themselves to obtain personal reminiscences. The value of oral testimonies lies in the truth of experience — of letting people speak for themselves about their daily lives and communities, their thoughts and feelings.

In these stories we see our mothers, grandmothers, great-grandmothers — ourselves. We see how far we have come and the hardships we have managed to overcome. The daughters of the early pioneers discuss their mothers' isolation and struggle in a strange society that speaks a strange language. Many women speak about the demands of being at once mother, wife and worker. Then there are also the stories of joys and accomplishments: the challenges of raising children and reaching career goals — of working in the Chinese Canadian community, organizing against racist media images or building a feminist artists' collective.

This book is not intended to be a comprehensive collection representing all Chinese Canadian women. Many women who should have been interviewed were not. Of the many women who were interviewed, over two-thirds of their stories do not appear in this book, especially the women who more recently immigrated and were interviewed in Chinese. We hope there will be a future book that will include some of the missing stories, further fill in the gaps and build on this first book.

The title of the book is *Jin Guo: Voices of Chinese Canadian Women*. The title comes from an ancient Chinese saying "jin guo is as strong as xu mei." This is a common reference to the belief that women are as brave and strong as men.

The Structure of This Book

Due to space limitations, we could not include the entire interviews of all the women. We selected nine stories which appear essentially intact. We feel that these stories represent a cross section of the women interviewed in terms of date of birth, place of birth, occupation, social status and current geographical residence. This section of complete stories begins with Margaret Chan, one of the oldest pioneers interviewed. Adopted by "relatives," she came to Canada at the age of eight and survived physical and psychological abuse throughout her life. This section ends with the story of Sharon Lee, a young, outspoken artist and writer, born and raised in British Columbia.

In order to present the stories of the other women in a meaningful context and tie in common threads we found woven through the different stories, we decided to lift excerpts from the stories and group these excerpts under particular theme categories, such as "Work, Work, Work!" or "Our Mothers and Fathers."

As we sifted through the pages and pages of transcribed interviews, we realized that many of the women shared similar experiences and feelings — sometimes even across generational boundaries. Certain patterns kept surfacing, especially around the themes of identity, marriage, parents and education. Even though some of the women claimed that they were not aware of racial or sexual discrimination, issues around sexism and racism are obvious threads in all the stories.

In the chapter entitled "Coming to Gum San," we learn about the feelings of isolation and loneliness experienced by May Mah, Shin Mei Lin and several other women upon arriving in Canada. Some of the women also talk about a downward shift in social status, a language barrier and the initial shock of facing their first Canadian winter. Others mention the lengths to which some Chinese had to go to gain entry into the country because of the Canadian government's impossible immigration laws: buying someone else's birth certificate, pretending to be a merchant — or paying thousands of dollars in Head Tax for one's family members.

The theme chapter, "Our Mothers and Fathers," includes some deeply personal reminiscences. Irene Chu, Valerie Mah and Sandra Lee speak with admiration and fondness about their independent and open-minded mothers. Other women, like Myrtle Wong and Lil Lee, talk about how their more conventional mothers gave obvious preferential treatment to the boys in their families. And others, such as Grace Lee and Dr. Linda Lee, discuss their estrangement from very demanding parents — and their ultimate reconciliations. Some of the women lost their fathers at a very young age or never really communicated with their fathers while others, such as Victoria Yip, developed warm, secure relationships with their more open-minded fathers.

The chapter on school experiences, "Education Was the Most Important Thing," shows us that Chinese Canadian women began rebelling against traditional attitudes toward women and higher learning long ago. Grace Lee, one of the oldest women interviewed, took the bold step of getting an education against her father's wishes, leaving her family in China and pursuing a teaching career in Canada. She claims that she never stopped learning, even when she was going blind. Almost all the women talk about a love for books — a love for learning. Some of the women mention racism in the classroom and the economic barriers to continuing their education. (In the first section of intact stories, Jean Lumb makes reference to actual segregation — a separate school for non-white children.) Many of the women mention the importance of Chinese school as a means of retaining the Chinese heritage. It is interesting to note that when the Chinese public school in Victoria was built in 1899, many of the students were girls. After graduating from Chinese schools, it was off to public schools. Later on it was the reverse, where elementary school was followed by two to three hours of Chinese school after class.

The most extensive theme oriented chapter in this book is "Work, Work, Work!" The title says it all. From a very early age, life has revolved around work for almost all of the women interviewed. As Jean Lee of Windsor recalls, "I was working even before I started school. I used to go down to the restaurant ... and stand on a box to do the dishes." The women who worked twelve hours a day beside their husbands in family businesses also had to raise large families at the same time — extraordinary cases of the classic "double burden." Those who worked outside of family businesses also faced racial and sexual discrimination. And immigrant women, such as May Cheung and Shin Mei Lin, found their lack of English a major obstacle to advancement in the workplace. However, the picture is, in general, looking brighter. Our interviewees included not only women in traditional fields of employment, such as nursing, teaching and factory work, but also a few lawyers, a writer, a municipal politician, a dentist and a stockbroker.

When we were going through the initial manuscript, we discovered some wonderful little anecdotes and descriptions of scenes — brief but vivid fragments or sketches which gave us a taste of the Chinese Canadian communities of the past. We have grouped some of these short descriptions under a separate theme entitled "Chinatown Vignettes."

The next chapter is "How Come You Don't Have an Accent?" The whole question of cultural identity and self image is explored here by a wide range of women — young and old, third generation Chinese Canadians and fairly recent immigrants. Some of the women speak candidly about painful childhood memories of "Chinky, Chinky, Chinaman." Many of the younger women who grew up here talk about their feelings of ambivalence — of feeling "in between." The resolution of this dilemma is found in different ways: denial, acceptance, creativity, political and personal struggle. As adults, some become more determined to learn their mother tongue of Chinese. Others stay away from the Chinese language and community altogether. But most achieve some kind of balance and are making an effort to pass on a cultural legacy to their children. However, it appears that some of the younger women are still searching for that elusive Chinese Canadian identity. As Anne Fong of Calgary points out, "It's really kind of a lifetime struggle."

In the chapter entitled "No Good-night Kiss — No Talk," we get priceless glimpses into Chinese family life, as many of the women recall how their parents and grandparents "freaked out" about interracial dating. In the case of Mary Mohammed, the Chinese community of Halifax ostracized her for almost twenty years because she married someone of a different race. Some of the Canadian-born women also discuss the cultural and communication gaps they have experienced in dating men from Hong Kong or China. And others speak fondly about how they met their husbands — and about the qualities that they value in a boyfriend or husband.

In the chapter entitled "Our Children, a New Generation," we have included comments about having children and raising children — along with comments about the future, our personal hopes and dreams. This chapter is very encouraging, as it suggests that the rigid gender roles imposed on little girls and little boys in the past have begun to fade. As parents, the women interviewed seem to be very concerned about giving their daughters and sons as many choices as possible. There is also a common desire to instill some knowledge of Chinese culture and language in their children.

Another very short, but significant chapter is "Coming of Age." Here three of the older women — Grace Lee, Victoria Yip and Anne Fong — discuss their feelings about aging and retirement. For these women, growing old does not mean waiting for death. Instead of slowing down and resting after years of hard work, they are enjoying their lives through travelling, exercising, going back to school, developing new hobbies, volunteer community work and meeting new people. Victoria speaks eloquently about the importance of peace of mind, faith in God — and acceptance. Her words on aging echo those of Madeline Mark whose full story appears in this book.

The theme section of this book concludes with "Speaking for Ourselves." This chapter covers not only women who have been involved in their local Chinese communities — women such as Ramona Mar and Rose Lumb — but also women who have represented the Chinese community outside of the Chinese community. Mary Wong of Hamilton was active in party politics and spent some years as a citizenship court judge. Valerie Mah has served on various advisory councils and committees. Tam Goosen is a school trustee in Toronto. And Winnie Ng has been active in organizing immigrant women factory workers for many years.

These are just some of the women whose words you will read in this closing section.

Setting the Historical Background

The history of the Chinese Canadians is an unfortunate chronicle of institutionalized racism. Much of the writing dwells on Canadian legislation against the Chinese community — head taxes for entry, starting at $50 in 1885 and gradually increasing to $500 by 1904, plus the 1923 Immigration (Exclusion) Act which prohibited Chinese immigration until 1947, making it impossible for Chinese workers to bring their families over at any price.

Immigration from China was essentially a male activity. During the 1850s, China was faced with famine, internal rebellions and the threat of Western powers bent on colonizing and sectioning off the country. It is not surprising that such a large number of Chinese men ventured to Australia, California and then to the Fraser River region of B.C. in search of gold. The earliest large scale arrival of the Chinese was in 1858 with the Fraser River Gold Rush. The next influx was between 1880 and 1884 when approximately 17,000 Chinese came to work on the final section of the Canadian Pacific Railway.

The men went abroad to try to make a better life. But this path of escape was not open to Chinese women. The male-dominated family clan put a lot of pressure on women to remain in China, instead of trying to follow the men. Some villages were supported entirely by the remittances sent by the family wage earners in North America. Thus, most of the women and children stayed behind to make sure that the men would continue to send money home.

The reluctance of Chinese women to emigrate during the late nineteenth century can also be attributed to Confucianism. Uprooting women and children meant the risk of severing village ties. The Confucian philosophy stressed the importance of the family and familial lineage. Harmony and stability within the family extended to the larger political and social environment.

The arrival of Chinese women caused a dramatic change in

what had been an exclusively male community in Canada. A wife symbolized economic success and status, since only the wealthy could afford the expense of bringing over a wife and supporting her here. Thus, many labourers, because they were too poor to afford a wife, lived their entire lives without marrying. In addition, the increasing numbers of women in the Chinese Canadian community signalled the possibility that some Chinese immigrants were not "sojourners" here temporarily, but immigrants who planned to stay permanently.

The majority of pioneer Chinese women came from the Pearl River Delta region of Guangdong province in Southern China. Women from this area have traditionally demonstrated an exceptional independence. The people of this region had been emigrating for centuries, mostly to Southeast Asia. So going overseas was an accepted practise and the strength of the family allowed villages to function in the absence of men. Women in Southern China have traditionally worked outside the home, demonstrating self-reliance by sowing and harvesting crops while the men were away.

On March 1, 1860, Mrs. Kwong Lee was the first Chinese woman to arrive in Gum San,[1] as Victoria was called then. She was the wife of a prosperous merchant from San Francisco. Immigration records show that by 1885, there were fifty-three Chinese women in Canada to 1,495 Chinese men.[2] Included among these early arrivals was Mrs. Cumyow, mother of the first Chinese child born in Canada in 1861.

Many of the early Chinese women came to Canada from 1885 onward. Most were merchants' wives. This increase reflected not only the growth of the merchant class, but also a response to the new fifty dollar Head Tax on Chinese immigrants. While not explicitly forbidding women to enter, the new tax made any further immigration extremely difficult.

Between 1885 and 1894, a total of thirty-four Chinese women entered Canada in the company of men listed as their husbands. Among these women, there was a noticeable age difference between husband and wife, sometimes as much as twenty years. One explanation for this age gap could be that these women were secondary wives. In China it was socially acceptable for a man to have more than one wife. Regardless of the number of secondary spouses he took, the first wife retained ultimate authority and importance. Often the first wife would remain at home to fulfill her filial duties to her husband's family while a younger wife would be chosen to go overseas.

The few women who did come to Canada during the nineteenth century were often viewed as "prostitutes" by the larger Canadian society. *The British Colonist*, Victoria's newspaper, contributed to this distorted image by publishing stories emphasizing the exotic and exaggerated evils of the Chinese community.

This distorted view was shared by the Women's Missionary Society of the Methodist Church which felt there was a need to "rescue" these Chinese women. They established the Chinese Rescue Home in 1886 to provide a safe refuge for prostitutes and *mui tsai* who were indentured servants often referred to as "slave girls" by white writers.[3] This rescue home was soon transformed into an orphanage and a school for Japanese and Chinese Canadian women. It also served as a home for widows and their children.

Most of the Chinese women who arrived in the 1880s and 1890s came to join their husbands or fiancés. For the overseas immigrant, marriage arranged through a third party in China was often the only means of obtaining a bride. After arriving in Canada, a great number of men had to postpone plans to return to China because of the expense. Instead, some of them arranged to have a bride sent over.

By 1911 Vancouver had replaced Victoria as the largest Chinese community in Canada. A missionary report of 1919 notes that there were 210 Chinese families in Vancouver which had a Chinese population of 6,000. This is in contrast to the 180 families in Victoria's community of 3,000 and Toronto's community of 2,100, including thirty-five families.[4]

Much of the traditional Chinese family life could not be transplanted to the overseas community. Although many of the women were free from the expectations and interference of in-laws, establishing a life in the new country demanded many sacrifices — and the sense of family took on greater significance.

Many of the pioneer women were thrust into an unfamiliar environment without the familiar village networks of support — without the language skills that would encourage interaction with the larger community. They were forced to deal with the double burden of racism and sexism in a white and male-dominated society.

While Canada was encouraging emigration from Europe, it was less receptive to those immigrants who, in its eyes, would compete with local labour and not assimilate. Because of the depressed economy, restricting "alien" immigration was an easy decision. In 1923 the Head Tax was replaced with virtual exclusion. The Chinese Immigration Act, 1923 effectively ended all further immigration of Chinese to Canada.

Chinese men in Canada not only faced the racism from employers, but also from trade unions who viewed Chinese workers as a cheap labour threat. Although Chinese workers at the turn of the century worked in places like fish canneries and organized themselves, racism forced them out of wage labour, except for domestic work as cooks or houseboys. They were forced to open their own small businesses in small towns across the country. Until quite recently, Chinese men usually had no choice but to work in restaurants, laundries, grocery stores, coal mines, or on farms. In the family businesses, women could always be found working side by side with their husbands or fathers day and night while still being responsible for raising large families.

Throughout the years of Head Tax, the Exclusion Act, the Depression and the two World Wars, daughters speak of watching their mothers working endlessly. They themselves often experienced a double load of work and school. Social life was very limited, especially when girls were subject to a much stricter set of rules than boys. For some, there was also the added stress of having to move around to where husbands or fathers were able to find work.

However, these hardships fostered a new and more intimate relationship between mothers and daughters. Many of the older women spoke little or no English and had few friends. In their isolation they turned to their daughters for comfort and help coping with the new society. Children acted as their mothers' eyes and ears — their communication link to the outside world.

Institutionalized racism existed at all levels. The attitudes which created the Immigration Act permeated through several layers of society. Chinese Canadians had no vote and were barred from certain professions. Educational opportunities, jobs and even housing were limited. Reading the words of these women, we were struck by the lack of bitterness or regret. What does come through, however, is their quiet resolve for a better life for their children and grandchildren.

During the first half of the twentieth century, the lives of Chinese Canadian women were both very tradition-bound and tradition-breaking. Some of them, like Madeline Mark and Victoria Yip, fought arranged marriages. Some even chose non-Chinese husbands in the face of tremendous prejudice from both sides. Others went against tradition and pursued higher education and careers (e.g. Grace Lee and Gretta Grant). And others, such as Jean Lumb, fought against the racist laws of the period prior to 1947 and helped to win reunification of families and enfranchisement for Canadians of Chinese origin.

The stories tell of a small nucleus of Canadian-born Chinese women who lived "normal" lives under abnormal conditions. They became involved in community and artistic activities, establishing lion dance groups and drum and bugle corps — and raising funds for medical supplies during the war years.

In 1947 the Exclusion Act was repealed as a result of pressure from lobbying groups in Canada, as well as from the international community. Chinese Canadian soldiers had just been fighting alongside the Allies in the Second World War. But even though the Act was repealed, the MacKenzie-King government still had ways of restricting Chinese immigration. Only children under eighteen, whose parents were Canadian citizens, could enter the country.

From 1950 to 1959, an average of 2,000 Chinese immigrated annually to Canada. Among these were young women in their late teens or early twenties who had come to join their new husbands. Decades of exclusion meant that many men married women who were twenty to thirty years younger than them. This huge age gap created another social phenomenon unique to the Chinese Canadian community: young widows with children to raise.

Some of the women who arrived during the 1950s and 1960s were ones who had been cheated out of the youthful years of their marriage due to the infrequent visits of their *gum san* husbands. When these women were finally allowed to join their husbands in Canada, they hardly knew these men. Because the women were in their forties and fifties, they were too old to learn the language or develop skills for the workplace. However, these women broke ground, paving the way for the women who came here after the 1960s.

The 1970s and 1980s ushered in a new era in the development of the Chinese Canadian community. At the same time a new flow of immigrants were coming from Hong Kong. Chinese women became involved in community organizing and politics. They produced literature and art based on their own experiences and diverged into professions which had previously been closed to them.

September, 1979 proved to be the turning point in raising the awareness of the community and making it more cohesive. The CTV program, *W-5* aired an episode that perpetuated racist stereotypes of the Chinese community. A national protest ensued and after several months CTV issued an apology. This incident led to the creation of the Chinese Canadian National Council for Equality, an organization committed to protecting and promoting human rights issues. Now known as the Chinese Canadian National Council, it has twenty-nine chapters across Canada.

Final Words of Introduction

Jin Guo: Voices of Chinese Canadian Women is a testimony to the strength, determination and spirit of the generations of Chinese Canadian women who made untold contributions to the Chinese Canadian community and Canadian society. We believe that these stories will inspire you, as they inspired *all* the women who worked on this project.

We are not claiming that this book is the definitive history of Chinese Canadian women. However, it is a first step in filling in a void in documented history. It represents a rich and diverse array of voices and visions. As noted earlier, there are common themes and ideas which run throughout the book, prompting us to make some broad generalizations about Chinese Canadian women. But making too many generalizations is, of course, dangerous, for it leads to oversimplification. It is clear that Chinese Canadian women have a lot to say and each of our stories is unique and multifaceted. An endless number of interwoven factors have come into play in our lives. We are neither passive victims of uncontrollable social forces — nor are we superhuman heroines.

The oral testimonies in this book provide intimate and honest insights into the lives of some very remarkable women. We thank all the women who were interviewed for sharing their experiences with us so openly and shattering the long silence. Your collective voices are a tribute to all Chinese Canadian women — past, present and future.

> Women's Book Committee,
> Chinese Canadian National Council

Notes

1. *Gum San* literally means "Gold Mountain," which the Chinese referred to first as California, then to what soon became British Columbia. Stories circulated in China that the streets of San Francisco were paved with gold.

2. Edgar Wickberg, et. al. *From China to Canada* (Toronto: McClelland and Stewart, 1983), p. 14. The RG 76 Immigration Records suggest that between 1860 and 1894, fifty-five Chinese women came from San Francisco.

3. *Mui tsai* literally means "little sister." It was a euphemism for a girl from a poor family who was sold to another family to serve as a domestic servant. Although she received no wages and was not permitted to leave, she was given food, clothing and shelter. In the overseas families, the *mui tsai* had almost a secondary

daughter status and the family she served had to find her a husband.

4. *From China to Canada*, ed. Edgar Wickberg et. al. Toronto: Mc-Clelland and Stewart, 1982, p. 95

INDIVIDUAL STORIES

0043416179

MARGARET CHAN

Margaret was born in southern China around 1902. She was in her mid-eighties and living in Vancouver at the time of her interview for this book.

Her story is historically significant because she immigrated in 1910 — a time when very few Chinese women came to Canada because of the racist Canadian Head Tax and the traditional Confucian views of the role of women. The "relatives" who sponsored her were probably very wealthy, since they had to pay $500 for her to come here.

Margaret was one of the first Chinese girls to go through public school in Victoria. She spoke about having to go abroad to teach because of racist policies which prevented her from teaching in Canada. She left when the Chinese Exclusion Act was in place. She had to return two years later because the Canadian laws placed this unique restriction on Chinese Canadians.

Margaret's story is also socially significant because she suffered so much as a child, and later as a wife, that she "ran away" twice. Hers is the story of a spirited survivor.

In 1989, three years after her interview, Margaret passed away in Vancouver. However, her words still live in our collective memory — and in our hearts.

Let's see, history not so to the letter. I will try and stick to the truth as close as possible.

My father was a gambler and he smoked opium too. He was not able to support his two daughters. So he gave me away. I became the adopted daughter of my relatives. My relatives brought me over to Canada when I was eight years old. They didn't treat me good, so I ran away. Treat me like a slave girl! I had to work and got no food. My aunty was not good to me —

always beat me, made me do all the work. My uncle was good. My aunty's so cruel. She didn't have time to teach me anything — my aunty was sick with asthma. Finally, they were going back to China, and they going to sell me to some people with a lot of children — so I run away to the Oriental Home.[1] I was thirteen and a half, maybe fourteen.

The Oriental Home was run by the Women's Missionary Society in Victoria. They saw the plight of the women in those days — under great suffering. That place could house forty-five people. Some of them were Japanese women deserted by their terrible husbands. So we all run to this home. It's called the Oriental Home — got Japanese and Chinese. It's like an orphanage. I, Margaret, was one of their occupants, and they helped me out immensely. We went to church three times a day then.

I went to school. I like learning things. I had to write the English exam three times to get my grade eleven. I had no time for friends during my school years — only school books. Oh, I got a few friends, but no time for friends when you are occupied already to pass the examination. My schoolteacher, Miss Martin, was my best friend. I got a few friends — they're nice to me. You got to have friends to survive....

After I finished grade eleven, I went to Vancouver to work in a fruit store, as a clerk, for about a year. Well, we worked hard — cold! Then we were half-starved. Worked in Canada Produce — not very good, I don't know. But we worked *very* hard. Never got money, and cold — worked overtime too.

Then I went back to Victoria to go to normal school (formerly a school for high school graduates preparing to be teachers). I worked very hard to reach my ambitions. I was the only Chinese girl among many girls and boys. I worked very hard with the help of the teacher in the Oriental Home, Miss Martin. She helped me with my preparation for my teaching course. Then, life is like a dream — sometimes you win, sometimes you lose.

After I finished normal school, I went back to work in a fruit store again. They paid $12 a week. No, that was not good! I borrowed $50 from Miss Martin, and went back to Hong Kong to try and get a teaching job. In those days in Canada, they discriminate against us Chinese. They don't give us a chance to teach here. I got my teacher's diploma, but they wouldn't give me a licence in Victoria, British Columbia.

I taught in Hong Kong, but then they didn't pay me enough. So when opportunity came along, I took a chance and went to Dutch East Indies (Indonesia). I taught in a multimillionaire's home, as a governess. I taught seven grandchildren and the millionaire's daughter. I was very lonely. They didn't pay me too much, so I went back to Hong Kong and taught in a village.

I was kind of lonely. But I had people that liked me — but then, sometimes it was not meant to be. When I went from Hong Kong to Dutch East Indies, I lost my good friend. That's my secret lover (laugh). He went back to Singapore. He was working on the ship — I met him there. I didn't marry him because, oh — I wasn't good enough, I suppose — wasn't beautiful enough. Well, I'm only an average woman. Beauty is in the eye of the beholder, eh? Right? I got some sense of humour. But he didn't want to marry me. He wanted common-law — who wants that? But we lose track of each other. He was wonderful, but then, it was not meant to be. I don't know — sometimes whom you're supposed to marry is predestined. Maybe I don't believe everything predestined, but then, I'm a cuckoo person anyways. My head does not listen to my heart. My heart say one thing, my head say another thing.

I returned to Canada on the boat, *Empress of Hong Kong*, in 1934. Depression time was really bad. I worked in a fruit store again. I lived in a place where the landlady was my matchmaker. She asked, "How come you didn't get married?" She introduced me to my husband who wanted a wife without having to pay. He came to Canada when he was eighteen years old. He tried to kid me. But I was foolish enough to marry him, thinking he never was married. He was older than me by five, six years. He was a cheater, fooled me because I was by myself — had no family here. When I married him, I was a working girl. I got some money. I sent $300 Canadian back to the village to his mother because I married her son.

I got married in 1935 in North Bay. We moved from place to place. When his cousin went to China, my husband took his job in Timmins. He worked as a housecook. I worked as a housemaid. So I have to go wherever he goes. But those days I was *stupid*. I should not have gotten children for him — I should have run away fast. There are other people like me, but I try to go the narrow, straight way, and try to behave myself — by being stupid as I was. I have too much hindsight, no foresight, you follow me?

Sometimes my husband's all right — sometimes not all right. I had nobody to back me up. Only God back me up. I not take everything for granted, because I'm not such a devoted Christian. But I fear God in so many ways, so many times. But God can understand us better than we can understand ourselves. We cannot understand our maker. God is our creator, and we are his creation.

I put up with my husband. He's a crazy maniac. When I was pregnant with the first baby, I sent $5 to his aunt. She didn't receive it quickly enough. He got a gun and shot at me — when I was pregnant! We were real poor when I married him.... I was scared. Well, to suffer and survive is something, eh?

I wasn't going to have any children, but then foolish me got one for him. My son, David, was born in Timmins, 1936. My daughter, Jane, 1939. Those days we didn't know about birth control. So when I stopped breastfeeding my son, I conceived a daughter. We learn a lot of things from our mistakes, eh? We sometimes learn, sometimes don't learn. But life is like a dream. You just can't make it the way you want it to come out.

After the second child, we sure don't want another child. I stopped having kids by using the common sense. They have some kind of ointment that stops the sperm before it can ... mate together. With the second baby I nearly had an abortion.

During my second pregnancy, one French lady told me to get an abortion for $25, but he's a quack doctor. You ask me why do I want to get an abortion? I got one baby crying on my neck — it's enough, too close together. But then, I don't know — I'm a coward. I'm scared of blood, so I didn't (laugh). With both babies I had hemorrhage. I thought, if you have an abortion, you die. I don't want to die. I don't want to die when I was young. When I was young I love to live. I'm old now. I don't mind dying — the earlier the better. But I don't want to commit suicide.

We just have so long to live. We can't tell God that we want to live forever. Nobody wants to live forever anyways. The tree grows old, you know. (Chinese: "You die early, then return early to the hills, If you don't die, then no road to take you to the next life.")[2]

Do you believe in reincarnation? Some people believe. But who are we to say we know what's going on? As I said before, life is like a dream, and it's a dream you can't control, eh? We all live on borrowed time, you know that? Every one of us, rich and poor, we all live on borrowed time. You borrow the money, you have to return it. God made us, and we got to go back to God.

In 1939 we left Timmins because his cousin came back and my husband had to find a new job. He went to Halifax to work, and I went to Vancouver with the kids. David was five and Jane three. I have two children on my hands — how can I work? We couldn't support ourselves — my husband got to support us. But for three months he lived with a white girl. He didn't send any money. I had a hard time.

I got very sick in Vancouver. My friend, Mr. Mah, took care of me. He's so good to me. I've got nothing to give him. I loved the children too much. Mr. Mah took care of me real good — but I reject him and went back to my husband, being the sort of faithful old dog that I am. It's not worth it sometimes. But who knows what's worth it then?

After I got better, I got a hold of my husband and told him we're going to Halifax to meet him. He loved the son, otherwise I couldn't have survived.

We wanted to rent a room in the hotel in Halifax, but they won't rent to Chinese. Discrimination was very strong at that time, before the war was over. The Second World War saved the Chinese here from destruction. They did not give the Chinese Canadian-born a vote. The government said, "You go be soldiers, and fight for your country." "It's not my country. You didn't give me a vote." So we fight for our rights, and now we've got the vote and everything.... But when we're all dead, nobody will remember a thing about us — all gone into history.

My husband worked in the Dominion Restaurant in Halifax, eh? He quit the job. Then we moved to Toronto. He must have earned some money in Halifax. That time he was really nice in a way, you know? I don't understand. He has a double personality.

One time good, one time bad — Dr. Jekyll and Mr. Hyde, you know?

I don't know everything. Sometimes I beat you one, sometimes you beat me one — like a game of checkers. I love to play checkers. I taught my son how to play checkers. When he was twelve years old, he had the measles and I wanted to keep him in the house. Then I beat him and he cried — and my husband threatened to kill me. I ran away to see my teacher in the London hospital. When I came back, my husband wanted to take the law in his own hands. He scare me to death, talking like that.

He always jumped down my throat whenever he got a chance. After being married to him for thirty-five years, it was time to take a leave of absence. You can't continue a marriage like that. I left in 1970, April, exactly thirty-five years.... He wanted to treat me like a dog — I barked at him and ran away. Any sense of humour in that? "Bow-wow-wow!" Can't take things too seriously. You have to laugh a little and cry a little — that's life.

You can't live with a man that will not listen to reason. You talk horses, he talks cows. You just got to run away from people like that — you can't survive. Life is short enough as it is, you know? As I said before, we all live on borrowed time — you understand now? He was not so mean in those thirty-five years because he loved his son so much. If I hadn't had a son, he would have thrown me away. I had a son — and now he doesn't want me, just wants his son.

You know, life is very complicated. You can't feel sorry for yourself. You should fight for your rights, and away you go! Run, like I did.

He wanted to take all my money. He's smart, but I am not too stupid either. Everything I took charge of — the children, baby-sitter, mother and sales ladies, buying savings bonds, and making payments for the house we bought in Toronto.... When I left him, I sued him for my share of the house, $8,000. The lawyer wanted $1,000. We bought the house in 1963 for $16,000. I wanted out — out, out, out! I won the case. He was supposed to support me with $55 dollars a month, but he gave me only one month. But I was not really healthy, so I didn't appear in court. So he hasn't supported me all these years. I get old age pension, plus the $7,000 I got from the house.

I ran away from him in 1970. I flew from Toronto to Vancouver after I won the case. After that he came out to try and get me back. I was staying with friends then. Now I have lived by myself in an apartment for thirteen years.

I can't live with my children. My children, they only behave when they need me — when they don't need me, gone with the wind, you understand? We didn't teach our children much. We spoiled them, let them have their own way. I don't know, my daughter's clever, but then, not clever enough — because the father didn't care for the daughter. He's old-fashioned. I was stupid not to love her more. That's why I always say I have too much hindsight, not enough foresight. But I was trying to gain my husband's favour and approval. I didn't treat my daughter as well as I treated my son. My son had asthma. I looked after him real good.

My son's a clever boy, high I.Q. But when I taught my son something, my husband always interfered. What can I do? He worshipped the son, but the son is a compulsive gambler now. But then, my husband spoiled him. He does not make use of his potential. I don't have anything to do with my son now. He kicked me out on my last visit to the house. He rejected me because I did not babysit their two children. Let bygones be bygones, but they have no forgiveness in their hearts. They treat me like so much dirt — I can't stand it! I got hindsight, no foresight. I should have known better than to go back there. I raised a son for someone else. If I were to die many deaths, it could never be as bad as going through that.

My husband expected me to take all that dirt — you know, I can't.... I'm a liberated woman — at least, I think I am.

When I came back to Vancouver, a friend found me a place to board for $150 a month. I lived there for two months. I moved because it's cheaper and closer to the shopping centre. The landlord at the other place was not very nice and not humane. Now only if they kept this place warmer, it would be beautiful. Well, the people have been very nice to me so far. They let me use my electric stove — I pay an extra $10. They're nice to me — only I'm not so nice to myself.

A lot of people have been good to me, you know. I'm lucky. Everywhere I go, there seems to be the hand of an angel holding me up, so I don't fall down and break my bones to pieces.

Notes

1. Oriental Home in Victoria. Originally established in 1883 as the "Methodist Home for Chinese Girls," by the Methodist Church, it was a refuge for young women seeking to escape a life of prostitution or contract marriages. The name was later changed to the "Oriental Home" for Chinese and Japanese girls and became a home for orphans and widows.
2. reference to Buddhist belief in reincarnation.

MADELINE MARK

Madeline is one of the oldest women interviewed for this book. She was born in 1904, in a little town in Ontario called Cayuga, about thirty miles from the city of Hamilton. Like many Chinese Canadian women of her generation, she spent many years working very hard in family businesses. Now retired, she loves to travel and practise yoga. At the time she was interviewed, Madeline was residing in Hamilton, Ontario.

My father came to Canada from China when he was about twenty years old. He was sponsored by his cousins and he had to pay $500 Head Tax. I remember that he wore a queue, you know, a Chinese braided pigtail. He had it wound around his head in our family laundry.

My mother was born here, but she was of French and German descent. She associated with three or four other women who had married Chinese men. And I remember that she used to practise some German traditions like decorating Christmas trees with paper flowers. She also taught us a few words in German.

My mother was about twenty years younger than my father. I think she chose him the same way I chose my husband (laugh). He was very kind and friendly, not like some men. But of course, her parents did not approve. No!

When I was growing up we moved many times — London, St. Catharines, Brantford, Grimsby, Toronto, all over Ontario. But we'd always land back in Hamilton. We got so used to it, we didn't know any different. My father would start a laundry business and then sell it, make a profit and then go some place else, dragging all of us with him. And no matter where we were, we always went to church every Sunday. My father was always the best dressed man with his bowler hat, brocaded vest and striped trousers.

When I was with English children, I felt just like them. My

father never spoke Chinese at home. He always spoke in English to my mother. We lived in Chinatown, so I could hear other people speaking Chinese, but I never really tried to speak it as a child. There was never an emphasis on Chinese culture in our family. But then I spent ten years with this lady named Dorothy Mo. She taught me a lot of Chinese.

When I was a teenager, I had many proposals from older Chinese men, not direct to me, but to my father. On a Sunday they would bring chicken and a bottle of whisky, things like that. I didn't know anything about it until they'd gone home. Then my mother would say, "What, what did they want?" "Oh," my father would reply, "They want to, um ... get acquainted with our daughter." My mother just raised Cain, saying, "Oh no, nothing like that, no!" And I said too, "Heavens, no!" I was going to business college then. I was only about seventeen or eighteen. My father said, "Okay, okay, it's all right if you don't want it." Imagine, a bottle of whisky and a roast chicken — that's just like selling your daughter.

After I quit business college, I worked as a seamstress in a tailor shop for about fifteen years. During that time I met my husband, George. He had his eye on me, you see. So he asked my father — who was semi-retired — to come and work for him at his laundry. One day George invited our whole family to come to his house for dinner. He wasn't like the other ones. He didn't bring us the chicken. He actually cooked the dinner. He asked us back for another dinner. Then he invited me to go to the show with him. Yes, he asked me directly. He was more westernized. He spoke English and had wavy hair. My mother said, "His mother must be English. He *can't* be all Chinese." I liked his ways, the way he approached me directly. He grew on me. I grew to like him, gradually. Oh, it took about three years (laugh). I didn't get married until I was thirty or thirty-one.

I helped out in the laundry business after getting married. They were starting to use electric irons then, instead of heating irons on a potbellied stove. I did the checking, the books, the tickets, the sheets, towels and flatwork. I also used to "turn the collars" because I was in the tailoring business before. Men used to wear out their collars, so I'd have a sign in the window, "Turn

Collars Free." You turn it over and it's like new again, see. I darned socks too. One man brought in twenty-four pairs of socks to be washed — with holes in every one of them!

I didn't go to bed until, maybe, two a.m. and I got up at seven every morning. I never realized until later how much work it was — the laundry business and raising five kids at the same time. But then, that was part of a bargain we made. My husband says, "Marriage is a fifty-fifty thing." It's really not. Sometimes you give eighty and he gives twenty, or you give ninety and he gives ten. Sometimes he gives more than fifty. It's an up and down thing. You have to give to make marriage work. I've been married for more than fifty years to the same man. And people said we wouldn't last six months! (laugh)

How did I ever do it — the work and the children? Well, I think it was love of my husband. I did my share and didn't question it. Those days were hard times, really hard. I knew that. I wasn't what you'd call a liberated woman then, but I am now (laugh). It's not too late, even if I'm in my eighties.

When the children were older we moved to Port Dover and got into the restaurant business. I worked for wages and was quite happy. The restaurant was on a main street where all the shops were operated by ladies, so we all got together. There was an art teacher on the second floor of one of the buildings and she held an art class for all of us ladies. I'd always wanted to paint. I loved it.

After three years in Port Dover we were back in Hamilton. We bought a hamburger place and called it Mark's Chinese Restaurant. Really nice — still is now, run by our nephew. We put all our money into starting the place, but it took three years to get it going. Then I worked eighteen hours a day, more than in the laundry. I began to think, gee whiz, is this all there is to marriage? Is this it — working, working, working? Never a holiday for the two of us. I decided to go on strike. I said to George, "No, I'm not going to go back and work for nothing all the time." I just didn't go to work. George got mad. I went back eventually, but I told him I wouldn't stay for sixteen hours a day. Then we hired help. We had waitresses. I still didn't get any money of my own.

I started feeling free when I received my first pension cheque.

Getting your own money gives you a sense of freedom, you know. I gave myself a party and told my friends, "We're going to celebrate." (laugh)

I think if my husband dies, I'll lose contact with the Chinese community because I don't speak Chinese fluently, and I only know Chinese people to say hello to. I am the last link to the Chinese heritage, since my children and grandchildren all married outside — you know, English or Irish. Life's been good to me as far as being half-Chinese. Some others have a hard time, but life is what you make it, regardless of your nationality. I can make myself comfortable with Chinese people and Canadian people. I'm proud that I'm Chinese, but I can adapt myself to Canadian ways — and I'm proud that I'm Canadian and I can adjust myself to Chinese ways. I didn't work on it. It just came naturally.

As the years go by, my life gets better. I started travelling after I turned sixty-five. I went to England for two weeks with my friend who's from England. I asked George and he said, "Yes, you got money, you go." He never paid for one cent of my travelling, not one cent. I've saved either from the rooms we rented out, or from money my children gave me. When you're working and raising children, you can't go anywhere. The only place I used to visit was my mother's home on Sundays. George would have his one day off and go downtown. He was a bit jealous of me going to my mother's. And he was a bit jealous of the children if I spent too much time with them — even now.

George never spent any time with the children. Of course a father's view is different from a mother's. When the children were growing up he didn't help out at all. I'd talk to him about the kids and he'd say, "Don't bother me with that. That's your duty. You look after the children. I put food on the table and a roof over their heads."

I'm in my eighties now. You take it from an old lady (laugh), don't worry about menopause. I didn't feel a thing. I stopped right there on my fiftieth birthday. No hot flashes or dizzy spells. I didn't feel that I became old. I was glad because I didn't have to worry about being pregnant anymore (laugh). I thought, oh good! Now it's better than ever ... even at ninety-two.... Oh, I'm pretty sure that's what keeps us both going! (laugh)

I grew up very sheltered, in a closed circle. School and back home, school and home. Church on Sundays and back home — that's all. Now I've broken out of that circle. I do everything! (laugh) Maybe I wouldn't be doing so much now if I had the opportunity to do these things when I was young. I keep very busy with my yoga classes and many other things. The only time I'm sitting still is when I'm watching *General Hospital* and *The Young and the Restless*. (laugh) When the commercials come on, I get up and do something else. I have no time to sit and feel sorry for myself. I don't have to feel sorry for myself, no.

I made our burial arrangements a few years ago. We've got the stone up, all written in Chinese. As the years go by, the gates are opening wider because the older you get, the shorter time you have to live. I started feeling this way about the age of sixty when my children were gone. I decided to become more active for myself — for myself. Before, all the work, everything was for the kids. I didn't think about myself as a person. But now I've decided to be as happy as I can each day, maybe by helping someone every day. I have no other duties or worries. I'm happier now than I ever was, more at peace with myself. When the children left home, I felt, oh well, I've done my duty. The Lord can take me. I'm willing to go any time.

WONG SIN

Wong Sin was born in Victoria, B.C. in 1915. She returned to China in 1921 and then immigrated back to Canada by herself more than forty years later. She has lived most of her life as a single mother since her husband abandoned her in China and went back to the States after the Chinese Revolution. She settled in Montreal where she worked in various factories. At the time of her interview, she was still residing in Montreal. Her story has been translated from Cantonese.

My family has been in Canada since my grandmother's generation. My grandfather came to Victoria to start a business. In those days there were not many Chinese in Victoria. I remember Victoria as a beautiful city. We lived in a wooden house with a big yard and lots of fruit trees. I remember the nuns coming to pick us up to go to church to pray.

I had four brothers and one sister. My father was not a rich man. He was a worker. My grandfather was in the grocery store business.

When I was six, my mother took me back to China. We were so happy because we had missed all the foods we couldn't find here, like peanuts and dried sweet potatoes. We went back to China because my brothers had become adults and it was time for them to get married. It was like that for overseas Chinese men in those days. Because of the scarcity of Chinese women here, the men had to go back home to find a wife. They couldn't marry a white woman. Chinese men had to marry *Chinese* women.

After we were back in China, we didn't like it. As small children, we were scared of the people because they seemed so different from us. And my mother would lie, telling us that they would grab us and eat us, so we shouldn't go too far away from home. China was not a good experience for me as a child. People called us names. And thieves thought we were rich. They came at night and tried to grab us. They called us "gold mountain girls."

We were very frightened, but we had to stay in the village because our mother had gotten sick and died soon after we came back to China. My sister-in-law was living with us, and when my four brothers returned to Canada, she became the head of the family.[1] Only the women were left behind.

My husband? Don't ask. He was an overseas Chinese living in the United States. I married him when I was eighteen. I didn't want to get married so young. Marriage is not free. He came back to China to look for a wife. When I married him, I left my own family and village to become part of his family, according to tradition. He left me in China a year or two later. Before he went back to the States, I gave birth to a boy. A few years later my husband came back and we had a girl. After the Victory he again returned to produce another son.

Life was good when I lived in his village with my mother-in-law. My husband's father was in the United States and he used to send us a lot of money, so I didn't have to work. I had a maid with me. We bought her as a child and raised her. We had some savings and we even had grain to lend to others. Many people died of starvation during those years of war with the Japanese. The Chinese suffered a lot. Fortunately, our family managed to survive quite well, even though we hadn't received money from overseas for many years.

After the war ended, my husband went back to the United States. He left me behind. We've been separated now for more than thirty years. He's never sent me any money. He's got another wife and family in San Francisco....

Life has many ups and downs. I was once a landowner, and then I went bankrupt. When the Communists came I was still buying fields. So they put restrictions on me for three years because I was a landowner. They took millions away from me. They checked on me when I was just going to the market. I had no freedom at all. I didn't even have contact with my relatives. Those were the rules. But I still had food. I lent people a lot of grain before, so I asked them to return the grain to me.

When I moved to Hong Kong in 1952, I had no thoughts of

coming back to Canada. I did some sewing for a church in Hong Kong. I worked night and day and earned $40 to $50 a month. We also depended on money my oldest son sent from the States. My life was poor. But I had been away from Canada for so long. Even though I had a brother in Canada, I didn't know English — so I decided not to return.

Then one day I met a friend at the market who asked me why I was still in Hong Kong when I was a Canadian citizen. According to my friend, even if I were forced to beg, it would be better to beg in Canada than in Hong Kong. That woke me up. I went home and thought about it. I was convinced it was the right thing to do, so I went to the Canadian Immigration office with a pile of documents.

When I first came here from Hong Kong, I wanted to take English classes, but they told me I wasn't qualified. I was born in Victoria! I was a Canadian citizen! So how could I not qualify? But I couldn't argue with the official. That upsets me — people who know English can get more money per hour. Whether you like it or not, you're forced to work in this society. Without a job, you have no source of income.

When I arrived in Toronto, I lived for about a month with my sister-in-law who's a Westerner. At that time she was living with her daughter because my brother was running a small business in a small town. I was used to eating only Chinese food, but my sister-in-law offered me crackers, hamburgers and bread — meal after meal. I couldn't stand it! One day my sister-in-law took me to Chinatown and I bought some Chinese groceries. Then no matter how much I cooked, my sister-in-law and her daughter finished everything. By the time I got to the table, there was nothing left. I couldn't go on feeding three people like this. I had only $20 left. I had no job and my brother did not know about my situation. So when Expo opened in 1967, I came here to Montreal to look for work.

I was fifty-one years old, so I was forced to work in a factory, cutting remaining threads off of garments. Not much of a chance of finding a better job. Later I got a job at an egg roll factory. I had never worked before coming to Montreal. My salary was $30 to $40 a week and rent was $30. I had to send money to my son in

Hong Kong, so that left no more than $10 for food. Life was difficult. One dime for thirty egg rolls.

I never went back to Toronto because the fare was too expensive. I had to spend according to what I earned. Besides, when you have to work all the time, you have no time to travel.

Much later I went back to work in another factory. For the first time in my life I made over $70 a week. My happiness only lasted a few months. I had an argument with the boss. I found out that he had a lot of money — but we, the workers, were the strength! He was making a lot of money from our labour! I was there to make a living. I was giving my labour in exchange for money. I said to him, "I shouldn't be deprived like that!" I had crawled out from the mouth of Mao Tse-tung. I wasn't afraid.... No, I wasn't fired because of the argument. Business was slow, so I was laid off.

My eldest son in Los Angeles phoned to ask me to stay with him and his wife. I went there for a few months, but they live on Hollywood Road on top of a mountain. That's where all these film stars live. It was too confining. Without a car, you couldn't go anywhere — so I came back to Montreal. Here I can go anywhere I want with a bus ticket or pass.

Back in Montreal I found a place to live close to Chinatown and a job in a garment factory again. Then the factory closed down. I lost hundreds of dollars because several pay cheques bounced. I had no job. So I collected unemployment insurance for a while until I retired and got my pensions.

In this society, the daughters-in-law will not live with the mother-in-law. My best daughter-in-law is the Caucasian one. She accepts things easily and is less picky....

I live in government housing now. You have to be living on a pension to get an apartment here. It's better here than renting a flat or a room. Here I am the head. When you live with other people, you're for sure under their rules and restrictions. Some landlords don't like you to use their phone or fridge. There's a distance between people.

I stay home every day. I cook when I feel lonely. Sometimes I read the newspapers, or go down to the malls like Eaton's, or take a walk. I always watch television programs or the video that my son bought for me. I've also learned a few sentences in English. But now with all my children living far away, I find myself feeling very lonely most of the time. It has been like this for a few years.

When I used to go to work, I wasn't lonely because I was so busy. You had to get up early and go to work. Then you came home and went to bed. Then the next morning the cycle started all over again.

Note

1. In southern China, it was not uncommon for many men of the village to go overseas. This meant that much of the work traditionally carried out by men became the women's responsibility — for example, farming. Thus, women often ran the households. According to tradition, the wife of the eldest son became the head of the family in such a situation.

JEAN LUMB

Jean was born in Nanaimo, B.C. in 1919. She came to Toronto at the age of sixteen and set up her own fruit and vegetable store. She has been a dedicated volunteer in the Chinese community since the 1950s when she was an instrumental member of the lobbying committee that went to Ottawa to appeal the Exclusion Act. For many years, she has owned and operated a restaurant in Toronto called Kwong Chow. She received the Order of Canada in 1976 and the Queen's Jubilee Medal in 1977. She continues to reside in Toronto.

I think a very important part of our history was the appeal for a change in the immigration law after World War Two. If it hadn't been for that change, not too many more Chinese would have come here. It was a long battle to get family reunion. We lobbied for ten years without even a hearing. But finally, the Chinese Canadians were brought together for the first time, united in their efforts to change the Exclusion Act. Delegates from across Canada went to Ottawa.

This happened during the Diefenbaker years. Since there was a Chinese Member of Parliament, Douglas Jung, we had a little stronger voice than before. 1947 to 1957 was a significant period because many people fled from Canton to Hong Kong after the war with Japan ended. Most of the women fleeing had husbands over here. They smuggled themselves into Hong Kong, but if our immigration doors were not open, they couldn't enter Canada.

A fairer law wasn't established until 1957. Before that the Chinese here were allowed only a C.O.D. bride. If you brought a bride over, you had to marry her within thirty days. If you wanted your mother to come, she had to be sixty-five or older. If you had children you wanted to bring over, they had to be eighteen years old or under. They kept giving us little changes, but not enough until 1957. The main thing we wanted was family reunification.

The committee to repeal the Exclusion Act was started in 1947 by Dr. S.K. Ngai, Dr. Henry Lore and Mr. Irving Himmel. Henry Lore was a Canadian-born Chinese doctor, one of the first professionals we had. Dr. Ngai came from Shanghai after the war. When he arrived in Canada he was shocked at the sight of the lonely Chinese men, without wives or families. They were just hidden away in what he used to call "little rat corners." He couldn't understand it. When he discovered that these men were separated from their families because of this immigration law, he started the appeal.

From 1923 until the arrival of Chinese immigrants in the late 1950s, there were very few Chinese children born in Canada, since most of the husbands and wives were separated. The men would go back to China to start families, hoping to bring them to Canada one day. Along with Dr. Lore, Dr. Ngai and Mr. Himmel, we had a true friend in Roland Michener, then MP for St. Paul's riding in Toronto. He was able to convince the Diefenbaker government that we needed to air our grievances. By the time of our Ottawa hearing there were twenty to thirty delegates from all over the country. Vancouver was supposed to be the headquarters for the Chinese Community Centre, so Wong Foon Sien from Vancouver was going to deliver our brief. The second speaker was supposed to be from Toronto, since we had the second largest Chinese community. I became involved because I was the president of the Chinese Women's Association for Ontario. Irving Himmel felt that a woman should speak too because this "Appeal for the Change of the Chinese Immigration Policies" involved the family. At first, they weren't going to include me because I'm a woman. I was the only woman on the whole board of the Chinese Community Centre. But Mr. Himmel insisted that a woman should go to stress the fact that we were asking for family reunion, not extra immigration.

It was a very successful meeting, even though we were all scared about speaking to the Prime Minister. The funniest thing was that when we got there, Foon Sien was seated next to Mr. Diefenbaker, but Mr. Diefenbaker insisted that I also sit next to him since I was the only woman delegate. Mr. Diefenbaker had one bad ear, the one next to Wong Foon Sien. So every time Foon Sien read from the brief, Mr. Diefenbaker would ask me what he said. Since I knew the brief inside out, I explained to him what had just been said.

The questions from the floor were mostly directed to me because of the fact that I was a woman and the issue was family reunion. It was just natural to have families together — how dare they keep our families separated? This meeting was the beginning of change, but it wasn't until right into the Liberal government in the 1960s that the change was carried through completely. I feel very lucky that I had the opportunity to be out front as an official spokesperson. Women have always had to be too much in the background.

We went through a lot during the period of immigration restrictions. Some people were selling papers. Say for instance, you had a son in Hong Kong who's eighteen years old, right age, but he doesn't want to come here. And I have a son who's twenty-one — too old. So we change papers, right? People were doing that before as a favour for a friend. So a Wong became a Lee, or a Lee became a Lin — like that. These poor kids had to lie about their age, their surname, their parents, in order to get over. Some were doing it for money. Some were caught later on. It brought a cloud of suspicion over the Chinese people. What a terrible mess. How could people go through the rest of their lives with the wrong surname, living in fear of being deported? There were also brides who came over with false papers. All kinds of complications! Some of these C.O.D. brides were being sold, brought over and channelled through another man and the agent collected the money. It all had to come out in the open.

I had to tell the Canadian government that if they didn't change the laws, there would be more and more people using false papers since they were desperate to come in. If you're desperate, you're willing to pay and lie and cheat, right? We wanted people to be able to come, stand up and say, "This is my *true* name and I have a brother, mother..." — or whatever. We wanted them to have a life here where they wouldn't have to hide. Finally, the amnesty program was granted by the Liberal government and all these people came forward. So our ten year fight was worthwhile.

The Chinese have a very strong history here in Ontario. When I came to Toronto from B.C. in 1935, at the age of sixteen, there were only about twelve or fourteen Chinese families here, but about two thousand Chinese people, mostly single men with families in China or Hong Kong.

I went into business with my cousin when I was only seventeen. We opened up a fruit store at St. Clair and Bathurst. My cousin and uncle paid my $200 deposit. It took me two years to pay it off. The store was called Wong Brothers — I was a Wong. Meanwhile, my father was not doing very well in Vancouver. He had a little pig farm and he was getting old. By 1937 business was good enough so that the whole family was able to join us. Things were better in Toronto. We opened a couple more fruit stores, called Wong's Produce and Sun Wong (laugh). Our entire family was in the grocery business.

In those days it was either the restaurant, laundry or grocery business. I had worked in the fruit store business in Vancouver, so it was the easiest type of work we could get into with very little capital and very little education. When we moved to Toronto it was mostly Italians who were in this business. During the war years the Italian stores were more or less being boycotted, as were the Japanese stores. Therefore, the Chinese people coming from Vancouver looking for new business in Toronto, found themselves in a very good position to buy out grocery stores from Italians.

We were told to boycott the Japanese people. But you have to realize that when we were growing up in B.C. the Chinese and Japanese went to the same schools. In those days there was still segregation for the "Others."[1] We couldn't go to a regular school because we were not white. I had to go to this school with six classes in one room — along with the Indians and "Others." We had to walk past the better schools to go to our Ward School. We did not pay too much attention to the boycott against the Japanese since we knew what it felt like to be the victims of segregation and discrimination. My best friend was still Japanese, although my parents would say, "You can't go into their store to buy candy anymore." We didn't have much money to buy candy anyway!

As a child in Nanaimo, going to a segregated school, there were many times when I had a terrible feeling of guilt or shame that I was born Chinese. "Why are we being treated this way? Why can't I do what other people do?" The most important thing at that time was being accepted into the circle. I didn't want to be outside looking in. I wanted them to accept me into this circle. Chinatown was considered a "ghetto" in the small town. We were put in one place, and we didn't come out of that place because that's where we were supposed to stay.

For a long time afterwards I had that terrible feeling that the English, the white people, were *fan gui* — foreign devils or ghosts, really bad people. That feeling stayed with me because the only time that the parents of these white kids allowed them to come to our Chinatown area was once a year on Hallowe'en night. On that night they had their masks on, with coloured hair or whatever. They came here and broke our fences down. They marked windows, drawing all kinds of very bad things. This is how we grew up, with our parents warning us, "Don't go down to the white people's neighbourhood because they're *fan gui*." So we learned to stay within our own little Chinatown area. We lived on one street with Chinese people all around us. It wasn't until quite late that we realized why we were scared — it was because of Hallowe'en night (laugh).

That's why when I was asked what I think of mixed marriages, non-Chinese to Chinese, I used to say that it couldn't have worked out during my parents' time. I didn't think my parents would be willing to accept it because they'd gone through so much, and they wouldn't want their children to be married to white people because of those feelings. But you have to understand that the only things that they knew about white people were bad things. Also, because of the Exclusion Act, men who were married already to women living in China would go and marry or live with white women. We always saw them as *bad* women. I mean, if they were *good* women they wouldn't live with a man who has a wife and children in China. In my parents' heads, the children of such mixed couples were half-breeds, not part of the Chinese society.

My mother chose my husband for me. I accepted my mother's choice because I trusted her. We were brought up that way. Even if the person wasn't what you thought he should be, you had to make the marriage work. Since we were not allowed to date or go out anywhere, how else were we ever going to meet someone compatible? In 1938 my mother said, "Jean, you're nineteen years old now and I think you should get married." My father agreed. In 1939 I got married at the Knox Presbyterian Church. It was probably the first Chinese *church* wedding in Toronto since most Chinese got married in their clan halls. My mother said, "Marry him" — so I married him — no questions asked.

Our family was very close when I was growing up. Early settlers in Nanaimo worked in the coal mines. Being a coalminer in those days was very different. When men left for work in the morning there was a chance that they might never come back again. The mine could collapse and you might never see your father or grandfather again. So life was a little more precious. You didn't take things for granted. Mothers would start the day with, "No children should cry. I don't want to hear anybody crying because your father's going to work." You had to stay happy. You didn't dare cry or make each other cry, or talk about unhappy things. When children are brought up like that, I think they have a much brighter outlook on life and appreciate each day more.

We never knew hunger as children — poor as we were. Although we were poor, we were never told that we were poor. My father used to say, "You can feed a family of ten on ten dollars a day. You can feed them on a dollar a day — you can even feed them on ten cents a day. It all depends on how you feed them." We were taught not to waste anything. We never minded wearing clothes that were pass-me-downs. We never minded that our parents couldn't afford something that we wanted. We never questioned and we never demanded the way children do today. I think that we were stronger. Earlier in Nanaimo the Chinese people had to cling to one another for support. We had to be strong because of the attacks from outside. I think this is what made families very united.

There is one generation gap between 1923 and 1947. We were straying away from the Chinese way of life. If it hadn't been for this influx of new immigrants, we would have been the lost generation. The change was so needed to bring the families together again. Now my grandchildren are going to know more Chinese because of the opportunities today as opposed to when my children were growing up. All of a sudden, there's more Chinese around — books, educational programs and even Chinese TV.

I had three years of Chinese school in Vancouver, but I learned more from growing up in Chinatown. My father was in the hotel business then. Every day we had to copy Chinese names in the registration book. Father made me do it to practise my Chinese.

The hotel was almost like a home since a lot of uncles and cousins lived there during the Depression days. We'd converse a lot with them in Chinese. Unless you use a language, it's lost. I think the fear of losing our heritage is very strong. It gets instilled in us that we must keep our culture alive. I can converse in Chinese, but more in a village dialect than Cantonese. I can speak very easily to the older people in my own dialect, but I'm actually more comfortable in English.

I sent my kids to Chinese school. I used to tell them, "When you grow up, you will never be able to say that you didn't have a choice — that you didn't have the opportunity to learn the language." I think my kids feel that they are better for it. They're not ashamed of being Chinese. If you have any inferiority complex, forget it. We are established — very, very firmly rooted. I feel that we have become accepted into this society. We don't want to push too fast. I've never wanted to stick out like a sore thumb. I just want to be a person to be respected. I think we've earned it — not just myself, but all of us. We've taken our place in the mainstream — and we're going to prove that more and more as time goes on.

You can look at the scholarship list in any school. If there are twenty scholarships, fourteen of them are bound to go to Chinese students. This is because we stress education as the top priority. We pass the message from generation to generation: "You've got to be better than better to survive." Here in Canada, with education we can become equals.

We are Chinese, so we're visible. A European could blend into this society without much notice, but a Chinese is a Chinese — even some of my grandchildren from mixed marriages. A man knows that if he marries a Chinese girl, he'll be using chopsticks at home. Mind you, as my father said, "Don't keep it all — only the better things from the two worlds."

Preserving the Chinese community has always been very important to me. In the 1960s I headed the Save Chinatown Committee in Toronto, a committee assigned to cope with what was going to happen to Chinatown when they took away the areas for the new City Hall and later the Holiday Inn. The big thing came when they were planning to widen Dundas on the south side, cutting our stores down to twelve feet of sidewalk. If they did that, it would have meant the end of Chinatown. You wouldn't believe the protest. We went into City Hall with forty or forty-five delegates from different organizations. Through our campaign they finally realized that Chinatown had to go somewhere. It couldn't just be wiped out, right? That's when the special Chinese committee, through the Toronto City Council, mapped out an area designated for Chinatown, from University over to Bathurst, and all the way north to College and down Queen.

Survival was something we learned from our forefathers. My grandfather was involved with building the railroad in British Columbia. Then in 1885 my father was brought over as a farm labourer in Nanaimo. Later on he worked as a coalminer. My mother was possibly the first Chinese woman in Nanaimo. She arrived in 1898 with my oldest brother. The remaining eleven of us were born here. Imagine, twelve children!

During the hard years of 1911, 1912, the government was already starting to push people to go back to China because of the labour unrest which was being blamed on us. The Chinese workers were getting less money than the whites, so we were accused of taking jobs away from them. When my father came, the Head Tax was only $50. Then it got higher and higher. Some men went back to China and never returned because they felt unwanted. Still, my father said, "There's hope here." At that time in his life, anything was better than his poor village in China.

The government thought that no more Chinese would be able to come if the Head Tax was raised to $500. But the Chinese people will do anything to bring a person over because that's the way we are. I think children in a Chinese family are cherished more than in a Westerner's family. My father believed that the most important thing in life was the person, the human being. So material things didn't matter to him. He could live in a two by four room and sleep on a board bed.

My father was very chummy and warm towards us. We'd complain that we were scared of ghosts, so he did something that not many fathers would bother to do. We used to live beside a vacant lot which local Indians used to visit. Because we weren't allowed to go out after a certain hour, we'd sit and look out our window at all these shadows going across. We were afraid. And every night, for I don't know how long, my father would go outside and sit on a rock and smoke his pipe. We would keep looking out the window to see how safe it was for him. We'd watch the Indians stop to talk to him. My father sat on that rock for many nights until we were convinced that there were no ghosts out there.

He was very good with his children, explaining things, never angry. When I was twelve he told me that I had to quit school and go to work. I cried that night because I was just beginning to enjoy and appreciate my new school in Vancouver. My father heard me crying and came into my room. He told me not to worry about leaving school because I was going to continue to learn at home and he would be my teacher. Using my older brother's books, I spent every bit of my spare time getting caught up with school. I learned so much more studying with my brother — and having my father beside me. He also taught me more Chinese than I would have learned at Chinese school.

I learned a lot from my mother too. We never realized until later how busy her life was. She was always pregnant. Twelve children in eighteen years. Even though she had such a hard time with us, she did teach us serious things about raising children. She knew how critical the first three years are — the importance of quality time. Talk to your children and spend individual time with them, even if it's only ten minutes. Mother was very gentle. You could ask anything of her. She never complained, except once in a while I heard her say, "A wife with a lot of children becomes a washerwoman, if we're not careful." She said that women should demand special free time or treats because we need it. She advised me, "Don't ask for too much, but it's important that we ask for some of the things we want — otherwise men don't know what we want. If I felt that for one day I would like some quiet time just for myself — without cooking or washing diapers — I'd let him know. Don't wait until you can't stand it anymore. Ask for it."

Sometimes we saw our mother really enjoying herself after the younger children had gone to bed. We used to have one of those old gramophones, and she would play Chinese music. Those were her private moments when she could just sit in the livingroom in her glory, listening to the music. She was almost like a different person afterwards. Meanwhile, my father was in the kitchen cleaning up the dishes and sending us to bed. It was amazing.

My mother and father talked to each other, unlike some Chinese couples. My father was always helping my mother cook while he talked about his day. And they always encouraged conversation from the children at mealtime, not everybody at once, but we all joined in. Those who didn't have their mouths full could talk and our parents were the listeners.

Mother was a very smart woman. She loved travelling. We would take her to the best restaurants, so she could get all dressed up. She deserved it. She was over eighty when she died in 1971. My father died in 1950. During her twenty-one years of widowhood, we took our mother everywhere and she loved it. She got the love of all twelve children. I wish I could follow in her footsteps and treat my children the same way she treated me.

I love my children, but I do respect my own privacy and well-being. In 1971 when we sold our house at Dundas and Beverly, we moved to this highrise — but instead of getting a big apartment for the whole family, I rented a second apartment just for the four children who had not yet left home. I simply felt that I didn't want to live with my children anymore. I wanted them to become more independent and cook their own meals, do their own house cleaning — I wanted to be freer. We had a very clear understanding. We have keys to each other's apartments but no surprise visits.

In 1982 I decided to gradually do less and less work. I had been working since I was twelve — forty years beside my husband in our family business. I wanted to start enjoying myself a little bit more. So that's what I've been doing. Today I have six children and nine grandchildren. I'm proud of being a Canadian.

Note

1. Segregated schools — The Victoria School Board segregated Chinese children in 1921, placing them in North Ward School. The following year Chinese parents withdrew their children from the public school system in protest.

GRETTA GRANT

Gretta was born in London, Ontario in 1921. Her father encouraged all his children to set high goals for themselves. Gretta attended the University of Western Ontario and Osgoode Hall Law School, University of Toronto. She was the first Chinese Canadian woman to become a lawyer. She has not only practised law and worked as a psychologist, but has also raised four children and served on numerous community boards, including the Chinese Canadian National Council, London Chapter. She still lives in London, Ontario.

I was born right in this city. There was quite a community of Chinese in London at that time but all men. The bachelors would meet at this so-called Chinatown at night and play *mah jong* since they had nothing else to do. Chinatown actually consisted of two Chinese food stores. Most of the men worked in restaurants or laundries. Once one person started a restaurant or laundry, the others would sort of follow. No matter where you went, you could find a Chinese restaurant in every small town.

My father had a restaurant and, of course, we hired only Chinese. The workers had living quarters there and they ate their meals there, so their entire lives revolved around the restaurant. I guess we were their family since their own families were back in China. Unless you were a merchant, you couldn't bring your wife to Canada. When my ingenious father found this out, he rented a stall in the open market and sold eggs and butter. Thus, he became a merchant and was able to apply to have my mother come over. The laws then were very discriminatory against the Chinese. Quite frankly, they were designed to keep immigrants out.

Both my parents had very limited education. My father could read and write, but that was about the extent of his education in China. I doubt that my mother went to school at all. She had her feet bound before she came to Canada. When my dad made her unbind her feet, they were so incredibly tiny. My mother told us that she was chosen to be one of those women trained to become a good wife. I remember her showing us a shirt that she had to make. She had to learn to spin and weave, sew and cook. She was never taught to read or write.

My mother never talked to us about the detention centre. The only thing my parents told us about was coming over in "steerage," down in the hold of the boat. The only thing they were provided with was water. You had to bring everything else yourself. It was the cheapest way to come over — below "tourist" class.

We all remember our mother with such love and affection. She did everything. She was an amazing woman. She raised eight children and managed very well. At one time she also had to look after my cousins because my aunt had died. She had an incredible amount of energy. I remember very fondly a dress she had made for me with a little bird embroidered on the front. All these little things we remember.

My mother was brought up to accept her position, her role. Her marriage was obviously an arranged one. She always appeared to be very happy because of the family around her. The whole family used to go fishing. My mother loved it. She'd catch more fish than my dad. And she'd always have a very nice lunch for us. She had all this organized — not just sandwiches but homemade egg rolls. She'd bring along her frying pan, the filling and a jar of beaten eggs and cook these egg rolls on an open fire while the rest of us were fishing. Can you believe this? She was just incredible — the things she would do for us.

My father was also a very kind person. Just to show you what sort of person he was.... When the Japanese were moved into London from Vancouver during the war, they weren't allowed to join the churches. I remember my father went to our minister and said, "Why, if you're Christians, would you not take these people in?" These people were Canadians like we were. And I think, if anybody should have any prejudice against the Japanese, it should have been the Chinese, since China and Japan were at war at the time, you know (laugh). But that's the sort of person my dad was. Well, the minister finally let them in.

My dad certainly believed in the Chinese traditions like honouring your parents, valuing family ties and that kind of thing, but he didn't like the superstitious belief in ghosts and bad spirits. I remember him saying that he was a bit of an upstart in his village. He and his brother came here to try and make a better life because he had no chance of going very far in China as an uneducated peasant. He was always working so hard.

We were once fairly well-to-do, and then the Depression came. At one time, my father's restaurant in London was the best known place for dinner. He had a little dance floor and Guy Lombardo and his band got started there. He opened that restaurant in 1914. I wasn't around then, but you talk to a lot of older Londoners and they'll tell you that Wong's Cafe was *the* place to dine with its silver-plated serving dishes and finger bowls. This was before the days of licensing places for liquor. When the Hotel London opened up and they were liquor-licensed, my father wasn't able to keep up. It became very difficult for him during the 1920s and 1930s. There were eight children and we all had to help him out after school and on weekends.

My dad believed so strongly in education because he knew that we needed it to get along in a very competitive society. He always said that you needed three things: health, education and wisdom. At examination time he would buy us fish, what he called "brain food." And we had lots of apples. He'd buy apples by the bushel.

We all felt a certain amount of security in our family and this is what gave us the self-confidence to overcome a lot of things. Who your parents are determines what you're going to become because of their aspirations and what they do for you. My parents were extremely hard working people. Even though they didn't have very much money and couldn't read much themselves, they always had books for us. What I'm saying is that my parents made a climate for us for education. The encouragement, support and money were there, although they couldn't afford to send us to school out-of-town. When three or four of us were going to university at the same time, there was not a lot of money available, so we had to pay it in dribs and drabs. You couldn't get student loans in those days.

One summer while I was in university, as part of the war effort, someone got the idea that the men should concentrate on military training and be relieved of menial tasks such as peeling potatoes and washing dishes. So they decided to get some female students to do these chores. Every morning we'd go by bus to the camp. They'd issue us these white dresses, big aprons and pith helmets. The commanding officer would march us from our tent to our various work stations. You could see us marching with these huge dresses and helmets. We used to just die laughing.

The following summer we worked in an airplane factory. We helped fix the bombers the men used for learning how to fly. Again they took a group of women from the university. They thought that we'd learn a little faster because we were university students. I was working in what was called "final assembly" where the planes came through for a final check before being shipped out for men to fly. There were about fifteen of us. We were guinea pigs. After we proved that women could handle this job, they hired a lot more women, and some became riveters. That was the first time they had women riveting in the factories.

We were the only Chinese family in our public school, high school and university (University of Western Ontario). But we really didn't face much discrimination in London. Because we were the only Chinese family in town, we were almost like a part of the community. Here was this nice Chinese family, you know, and they kind of took us to their bosom (laugh). If you're the only ones, there isn't the same discrimination as there is when you have a lot of Chinese in an area. Once you get a large population, people tend to fear the group.

Luckily we were able to do fairly well in school. We were able to achieve. That helped. If you're Chinese, you have to do better to be accepted. My father instilled this message in us. Because he could foresee some prejudice out there, he used to say, if you're going to do something, you have to do it as well as you can, if not better than your classmates. He also encouraged us to get into professions where we could be our own bosses. That's why two of my sisters and one brother went into medicine. My other sister became a biochemistry professor and I chose law.

When I came to Toronto to go to law school, it was like a whole new world for me. It was the first time I really encountered prejudice. Toronto had a big Chinese community compared to London. But there was more segregation. The non-Chinese wouldn't accept you as much as they did in London. And the Chinese didn't accept me as much either because I couldn't speak Chinese very well and I appeared to be more aggressive and athletic than most of the other Chinese women. However, I did get a lot of dates, but that's beside the point (laugh).

In Toronto both the Chinese community and the non-Chinese community expected me to date Chinese men. If you showed up with somebody who wasn't Chinese, they'd look at you different-ly, even though they were still your friends. There was discrimina-tion in the university sororities as well. This friend of mine knew I really didn't want to join, but she wanted to test the tolerance of her own group. So I agreed to go through the process of applying. Eventually, they accepted me, but there was some discussion about whether or not they could let in "coloured." Then I turned them down (laugh). That would be about 1941.

When I was growing up, we didn't speak Cantonese, just a local dialect. There was no Chinese school for us in London. I think my father felt badly about this. He hired a private tutor to help us with our Chinese, but it just went by the wayside because we were so busy with all the other things and my parents were both trying to learn English. Now I can't speak Chinese at all. I married a Scottish Canadian. My oldest brother married a French Canadian. At that time interracial marriage was really frowned on, but it was okay with my father. He was more open-minded than most Chinese. My youngest brother married an English girl. Then another brother married outside of the Chinese community as well. My younger sister married a Japanese man, so only three out of eight children married Chinese. My father preferred that we go out with people whom we enjoyed socially, philosophically and intellectually, rather than go out with a person just because he was Chinese.

When we were teenagers we used to have a steady stream of Chinese visitors because there were four girls and four boys in our family. Any Chinese from Nova Scotia to Vancouver who hap-pened to be looking for husbands or wives would come to our house every summer. I remember one of my older sisters was away and this chap came by with his parents. His mother said, "Oh my, you have such a good-looking family, and my son isn't good-looking, but we'd like him to marry..." (laugh), and they'd try to pick out the most appropriate girl from our family. I remember writing to my sister, "We've got this guy for you." (laugh) I remember almost being ill because some older man came up to me and he said he was going to ask my father if he could marry me. I ran to my mother and said, "Don't you dare!" (laugh) In those days, a lot of that sort of thing was done, but my dad would never force us to marry anyone. He felt that we should have freedom of choice.

My husband, whom I met at law school, came from an immigrant Scottish family, the Grants. He was intelligent, kind and thoughtful, and going through for law — the apple of his parents' eye. No girl was going to be good enough for him. And then I came along (laugh). There was no difficulty at all with his father, but I'm sure that his mother would have preferred a non-Chinese for her son. However, once the ice was broken, Mrs. Grant was fine. My in-laws were as kind and accepting of me as we could have ever hoped for.

I have one daughter and three sons. There are always going to be some difficulties for children of a mixed marriage. As with anything, you learn to help them cope and overcome obstacles. As an example, when our children were growing up, somebody would say, "Where did you come from?" You see, two of my children look very Chinese while the other two are sort of in between. So we taught them to say, "Well, we're Chinese Canadian, and what are you? Holstein?"(laugh) We decided we'd equip them with one-liners to be able to disperse negative feelings, make everybody kind of laugh.

The most discrimination I've ever felt was from the Hong Kong Chinese who seemed to look down on us as colonials, not being able to speak Chinese. I met a group of them at a conference one summer at Yale University. They treated me like a second class citizen. Because I would go up and talk to anyone instead of holding back as they did, these Chinese women at the conference thought that I was being too aggressive. They didn't even consider me Chinese because my whole manner was different. I believe that this kind of attitude still exists. When my daughter was going to university in Toronto, the Chinese women students would be very nice to her on a one-to-one basis, but when a group of Chinese-speaking students came along they'd go off and speak Chinese and ignore her. She always felt cut off from them.

After I finished law school I went back and took psychology. Then I worked in Corrections. Soon after that I got married and worked as a psychologist. Then the children began coming, so I stayed home for a while until my husband started encouraging me to get back into law.

Both working at home and outside of home have been positive experiences. In my day it was easier to leave your profession temporarily to stay at home and raise your children. But now, some woman professionals are afraid that they won't be able to get back into their field because of the competition for jobs. If you have a very good position, you may not wish to give it up. Then some women just don't want to stay home. That's an option too.

I see some professional women who are under a lot of pressure because they take their kids to daycare. They have full-time jobs and then they have to go home tired and be a parent. I think it can be done, but you have to have a lot of help at home. Although we are legally "equal," we still have the greater burden — unless you're very lucky to have a husband who can assist in everything or you can afford a nanny.

My husband kept urging me to get back into law because he had great respect for my ability. Obviously however, there were a lot of men at that time who didn't think that women should be in law. I remember some of the older lawyers would say, "No, here dear, I'll help you do this." And I let them do it. There's no point fighting with them. I'd just say, "Fine, thank you," and I'd watch them. If they didn't do it right, I'd say, "Now, I'd like you to change that." But I wouldn't antagonize them. I think if you are too aggressive at first, then they get frightened because men have a great difficulty accepting "an aggressive woman," or one who's out in the public and confident doing things that they think women shouldn't be doing. I think you have to gain their trust first, and then things are fine.

I was very fortunate because I articled with one of the big firms in Toronto, McCarthy and McCarthy. At that time there was some prejudice against Orientals, certainly towards Blacks and Jewish people as well. Some of the big firms wouldn't take Jews. There was one Black lawyer, and he was only able to article with a Japanese Canadian firm.

When I returned to London I got involved with the Local Council of Women and the Women's Canadian Club. Then I was on the boards of International House, Fanshawe College and the John Howard Society. Being a lawyer and being in legal aid, a lot of people asked that you become a member of their board. So over the years I've served on many community boards, including the Children's Aid Society and the Child Abuse Council.

I'm sorry that I can't help out in the Chinese comunity because of the language barrier, but I'm still trying to find a way to get involved. A lot of us Canadian-born have lost the language, but I think you can still maintain your cultural heritage without having to learn the language. My children know that I'm Chinese and that they are different from me, having the background of two cultures. They know that it's necessary to preserve the link and keep the Chinese and Scottish cultures alive. There are more and more mixed marriages today. Children are inheriting many cultures, which I think is interesting, but putting all that together can be really challenging.

Chinese Canadian women bring a different culture to the society. I don't think we should be completely assimilated. Like any other group with something to offer, I think we should be integrated into the community, to take part in it and maintain our Chinese heritage at the same time. Assimilation means giving up everything. We should all increase our awareness and under-standing of other cultures. People should not look at me and say, "Oh, you come from China where they bind feet." I'd like people to remember that China is an old civilization with a rich history in the arts and sciences. We should take the best from each society.

I'm over sixty-five now. I think that facing retirement is one of the biggest challenges. I have to learn to let go, just like I had to know when to let go of my children. The future? I just want to work for as long as I can and be a wonderful grandmother!

KIM

Kim is a pseudonym for a woman born in southern China in 1937. She immigrated to Canada in 1957, as the bride of a Chinese Canadian who had returned to Hong Kong to find a wife. At the time of her interview, she was residing in a small town in the Atlantic provinces. Her story has been translated from Cantonese.

Our family was very feudal. My father was the third-born in his family — but he was also the only son, so he was considered the eldest. Because my father was so feudal in his thinking, he was very filial. My grandfather wasn't there, so my grandmother had all the say. Oh Grandmother was so fierce!

Grandmother had bound feet.[1] Her feet were so small, like the size of my palm — just like tops. She couldn't walk fast. Her toes were all curled up, like they were braided. The cloth she bound her feet with was long — yuck, so smelly! She would take it off at night for washing. My father was so filial that he made us young ones kneel down to help her take off the cloth, wash and then rub her feet. Then we had to give her a clean cloth, and she'd bind her feet herself. No one else knew how to do it.

Grandmother wouldn't let us go out to play. She said that girls shouldn't go out. Every day when we finished school, we had to go and tell her, "Grandmother, we're back." And she would say, "That's a girl. Go and do your calligraphy and recite your books." That would make her happy. If you picked up a ball or rope to play with, oh, oh, you were in trouble! She'd say to my father, "Those girls, their feet are so big! They don't bind their feet — such a disgrace!" But by that time, after the Liberation, footbinding was no longer fashionable. When our grandmother died and we were grown-up, it was like being discharged from prison.

Our family was very strict. We were not allowed to talk during meals. When you finished your rice, you had to hold up your bowl and say to everyone, "Please continue everyone." My father ate with my grandfather while my mother and older sisters and I ate together in another room. No, my parents never sat at the same table and I don't remember them ever going out together.

My mother had over ten children, but only eight survived — four boys and four girls. The boys were, of course, number one and the girls nothing. The girls never got any inheritance. They said this is because girls would marry out to others and become part of someone else's family. The boys carry on the family name, the ancestral line. Girls were disadvantaged in every way. On the wedding day, as the bride stepped out of her parents' house to go to her in-laws' home, she had to sing some songs, crying real tears as she sang.

It was bitter because after marriage a girl became like a servant to her mother-in-law. In the old days, if you wanted to visit your own mother's home, you had to ask your mother-in-law for approval.

I met my husband when he was studying at my father's school. He was a very good friend of one of my brothers. After his father took him to Canada, we kept in contact through letters. In 1954 after the Communist victory, I left southern China for Hong Kong. A short time later we met again in Hong Kong. He had come back to get married because his family didn't want him to marry a white girl.

Before coming to Canada, I sometimes read about this country in magazines. And from what my husband told me, I knew that language would be a problem since there were hardly any Chinese in the small town where he lived in the Maritimes. There were only four of us Chinese women, including my mother-in-law and myself.

In those days I was so dumb. I didn't know a thing. Others talked about "enjoying the honeymoon." I was too young and inexperienced at the age of twenty. I had no feelings when I arrived in my husband's town in Canada. It was like being imprisoned. My husband came to Hong Kong during a school holiday to marry me and bring me over here. One week after we came to Canada he had to go back to school in another city, leaving me alone with his parents whom I had never met before.

Before marriage I never had to do anything but go to school. I had servants to do things for me. When I came over here I had to do everything myself. I was miserable. I didn't know how to wash the clothes, just kept rubbing them until the skin came off my hands.

The overseas Chinese here were so thrifty. Nobody would pay others to wash clothes. All of a sudden, you have things piled up for you to do. If my family had been in Hong Kong, I would have flown back.

Racial discrimination was severe in the small towns around us. Where my cousin lived the people wanted to form a group to build houses. At the beginning everyone was quite enthusiastic, but when my cousin went to join, people started to withdraw one after another. They didn't want to be in the same group with a Chinese person. Then he withdrew and they all started to join again. That's discrimination.

Many Chinese who came to Canada in the 1950s had to falsely claim someone as a father. In Vancouver a fellowship association was formed, so that if any Chinese came, someone would go and claim that person. Once the newcomers paid the Head Tax to the *gui lo* at Immigration and someone came to claim them, they were let go. If no volunteers from the fellowship association were available, some of the newcomers had to stand there and wait for a day or two until they were claimed. There were also long waits sometimes for the medical examinations, depending on the number of immigrants arriving that day.

My father-in-law used to talk about the "pig house" where immigrants were detained like prisoners.[2] When you went to the toilet you'd be followed because they were afraid you might escape. When my father-in-law came, it was winter and he didn't have enough clothes on. There was no rice, just bread. He couldn't eat that, so he suffered from hunger for two days till he was claimed.

If a woman came, she'd have to disguise herself as a man. There was an old woman who told us that she disguised herself as a man by braiding her hair and wearing the black cap that Chinese men wore in those days. They didn't always check you closely. You just paid the Head Tax and you could come in.

Not many Chinese women were here — I was mainly aware of those women who were brought over to satisfy the physical needs of the overseas Chinese men. Some people in the prostitution business would go back to Hong Kong and buy the women there, have them disguised and pay their Head Tax to come. I heard those people say they made a lot of money.

Later on, my father-in-law sponsored a lot of the overseas Chinese here. None of them knew English and they couldn't work for the *gui lo*, so we had to open up a restaurant, giving them jobs in the kitchen. My husband and I began to help out at the restaurant. I mostly waited on tables and did the cash. Working in the restaurant was very busy. You could only leave after the last customer left, and you had to start work early in the morning. The Chinese in our town all ran restaurants — only one was in the laundry business.

Many of the Chinese here were illiterate. Since he could speak some English and knew how to run a business, my father-in-law was considered very smart — although he couldn't read or write. Those days people called out orders, instead of writing them down. One time, someone mute came in and wrote down the order. It was early in the morning before the waitress arrived. So my father-in-law took the piece of paper with the order on it and stood outside until a *gui lau* passed by. He asked him to read it out: "bacon and eggs, sunnyside up." One's "blind" and one's mute — what can you do? Life was so hard.

My mother-in-law also helped out in the restaurant. She didn't like the work, of course. These *gum san* old women of my mother-in-law's generation lived in luxury before coming to Canada. Back in China they didn't know how hard the old men worked here. One hundred Canadian dollars could be exchanged for several hundred in the village. They thought they had so much to spend. But who knew that after coming here, you'd be in front of a wok or a pile of clothes all day just to make a few dollars to send home.

There was no such thing as a day off. We really worked 365 days a year. No one questioned how much they got paid. I talked to an old man yesterday who never bought himself any clothes, always wearing the few pieces he had until they were totally worn-out. Women were the same. In those days there was no such thing as fashion. The new immigrants today talk about travelling, but we never went anywhere. Our only entertainment was gambling.

I liked to play *mah jong*, but it took a lot out of me since I had to go to work so early in the morning. I wanted to quit, but it gets addictive! It's mysterious. If you didn't play it, you didn't have many other opportunities to socialize with other Chinese. Once you start playing *mah jong*, you forget things. We play big — one round can be several hundred dollars. In one night you can lose $700. It's nothing. You don't even blink. If I didn't play I don't know how much money I'd have now. I've lost a lot, but sometimes you feel that it's worthwhile because you feel so relaxed afterwards.

Living conditions were not very good in those days. The buildings were run-down. There was electricity and running water, but the water was like a thread. I didn't really want to go out. The whole day I spent either in our home upstairs, or in the restaurant downstairs. It's too depressing talking about these things.

I still feel imprisoned here. What's so good about our life in this country? We've lost our traditions and customs — and you can't do anything about it. Now I can speak and read some English. And it seems like I can mix with the *gui lau*, but actually it's just superficial. No real friends.

I don't know when I started getting used to the isolation and being taken advantage of by my husband. We were not as smart as girls nowadays who can say when they want or don't want to have babies. The year after we got married I gave birth. How miserable when you don't know how to take care of babies. My in-laws had only one son, so they did not think that two boys and two girls were too many.

They waited a long time for a third grandchild after the first two were born. My mother-in-law pushed my husband to see a doctor. He was too embarrassed to argue with me, and I was to embarrassed to talk to him about it. When I did become pregnant, he was very happy. My husband was spoiled as the only son. He just did whatever his mother told him.

When my mother-in-law was in China, she was able to hire

other people to take care of her babies for her and serve her. Living in Canada, I became the person to serve her. I was always at her beck and call. Of course, I followed tradition because I was from a feudal family. Before I got married my father had already instilled these ideas into my head.

Here the *to sang* (native-born) can't accept it at all when we are talking about old times. The talk of old times is too abstract for them — you know, like Chinese New Year and village festivals.

The children here are much stronger and bigger than those in China. Of course, there's a bit of a communication problem with the children. We still have all the old thinking in us, to respect the old and to be polite to others. The *to sang* here talk back to us with a "why," and say "I can make my own decisions." They argue with you until the end. Their customs are all Western. No, I wouldn't want to live with my children. The children wouldn't want me anyway. The generations are different. I have lived with my mother-in-law, so I know. It's the thinking that is different. You like something and they like something else. If you live apart, you visit each other like friends. That would be much better.

Notes

1. Footbinding was practised among the wealthy class. Girls had their feet bound from the age of seven, crippling their feet. Bound feet were a status symbol and were considered erotic.
2. "pig house"/detention centre — the immigration building built in Victoria after 1907. Resembling a prison because of the thickness of its walls and the bars on the windows, the Chinese referred to it as the "pig house." Chinese and South Asian immigrants stayed here from a few days to months before they were permitted to land. Those who failed the medical test or the interrogations were returned to their home countries. Vancouver also had an immigration building referred to as a "detention centre" or the "piggery."

ROBERTA MERCER
and
JANET TRIFA

Roberta (b. 1954) and Janet (b. 1956) are two sisters who were born and raised in a small town in Saskatchewan called Leask. Their family was the only Chinese family in town. At the time of their interviews, both women were living and working in Saskatoon, Saskatchewan.

JANET

Our family name is really "Mak." Grandfather's full name is really Mak Hun Sun. There was an old Scottish guy in town who would always tease him and say, "Your name is not 'Mak Hun Sun' — it's 'MacHanson'!" Then because our grandfather was in business, a lot of companies would kind of join the Mak-Hun-Sun together when they wrote his name, until it eventually did become "Mac-Hanson." Some of our dad's brothers still go by the name Mac-Hanson, and some by the name Mak. The two of us were born as MacHansons.

ROBERTA

Dad's father came to Canada about sixty years ago. We don't know much about our grandparents because our grandfather passed away before we were born, and our grandmother passed away when we were still very young. I remember her as a very jolly, easy-going lady. Although she had twenty-one children, she seemed to have time for all of us.

A few years ago, Mom, Dad and I visited China. It was the first time my mother had seen her mother since she left China as a teenager. She's now in her fifties. My impression of my grandmother is that she was living all that time to see her daughter again. It had become her whole purpose in life. When she saw my mother she said, "Now it doesn't matter when I die because I've seen my daughter again." She was very happy to see me too, but she was disappointed not to meet a grand*son*.

Our mother came to Canada around 1950, at the age of seventeen. She was very strong. Anyone who can leave her family and homeland at such a young age, knowing that she may never see her family again, would have to be an awfully strong person. She met and married Dad in China when he was sent there by his father. He returned to Canada first and she joined him a year later. Dad owned a hardware store, so Mom always had to work, plus take care of us kids. Somehow she still managed to have time for us. She was always there whenever we were sick. There were the two of us and a brother. She gave birth to two other kids, but they passed away as infants. She had all of us close together. She was maybe twenty-eight when she had the last baby.

JANET

Mom never talked to us about birth control. When we got to the age when girls first start to have their periods, she didn't really explain too much to me. She just said, "When you see blood on your underwear, just tell me." And that's all she ever said about it.

ROBERTA

I think both our parents just shied away from topics like that. They were never very open in front of us. No signs of affection or anger. They never fought in front of us. We had never seen our parents kiss until their twenty-fifth anniversary when we held a big party for them, and we all banged our spoons.

JANET

Yes, that's one big difference between the cultures and between generations. My husband's very physical, whereas with Mom and Dad, we just never...saw that. We just didn't feel comfortable going to our mother to talk about boy-girl relationships. It was all kept hush-hush. I found out most things through friends whose parents must have sat down to explain everything to them. I think it would have been nice to hear it from one's mother, because you didn't know for sure if what your friends were saying was right or wrong.

But I really admire our mother, especially when I think back to what she's gone through. Yeah, she's pretty amazing. If she was sick, she would still go ahead with her daily work routine. Because we had living quarters at the back of the store, she would be doing things in the back, like cooking, and if she'd hear customers come into the store, she'd go out and wait on them. When she first came over she did not speak any English, but she had no choice but to pick up the language, since we were the only Chinese family in town.

ROBERTA

Mother had come from a fairly wealthy family. She never had to cook and she used to be a very fussy eater. All of a sudden, when she came here, she not only had to cook, but she also had to look after children, work in a store and learn a new language. She was just thrown into all these new things that she never had to face before.

JANET

And she never complained. We never heard her complain.... Mom and Dad never took holidays when we were young. It seemed like they would work, work, work, to save money just for us, their three children.

ROBERTA

Mom and Dad are still very active. Although my brother and his wife have moved back to Leask to help them in the store, my parents have not retired. They'll work in the store for as long as they live.

I have a hunch that Mom could have fallen into a sense of isolation in Leask, but I think Dad forced her to get out and socialize. He would take her golfing or curling and encourage her to go out for coffee with the ladies. Now on weekends they'll invite friends over to play cards. Then there's the other Chinese family in a town seven miles away. Because of the scarcity of Chinese people in the area, this family has become like family to us.

This is generalizing, but Chinese people seem to have a stronger family bond than a lot of Canadians. They seem to show a greater respect for their parents. My mother still looks out for her mother, sending her money overseas.

JANET

I think we grew up with a feeling that we were very important to our parents. There was never any insecurity about their love. Recently I've found in talking to my Canadian friends, they don't have that same feeling of emotional security with their parents.

Our parents always stressed the importance of going to university or college. They didn't push, but they were very supportive. Mother went to a private school in China. Father went to Toronto to take a radio electronics course after high school.

ROBERTA

I generally enjoyed school. I found that I got along really well with the kids at school — in fact, to the point where I thought I wanted to lose my own identity. I wanted to be just like the other kids. I didn't want to have anything to do with my Chinese culture.

JANET

Do you mean you wanted to be white?

ROBERTA

Yes. I didn't want any Chinese part of me to show. The kids accepted me, and I thought it was because I was just like them, but I didn't realize then that they were actually accepting me for what I was. I didn't want to stand out as different. I resented having to eat rice. I swore that when I grew up I would never eat rice again — because no one else I knew ate rice every night (laugh).

It's surprising how this attitude stayed with me for a long time. I really don't know why, because it wasn't as though the kids ostracized me for being Chinese. Once in a while you'd have the experience where somebody would call you a name like "Chinky, Chinky, Chinaman!" out the school bus window. Such incidents would set me back for a long time. I think I was a lot more sensitive than Jan was.

JANET

Being Chinese didn't bother me. But as I was getting into my teens I had really bad acne. I was always hung up about my acne and my size, so that took me away from dwelling on my Chineseness. People liked to tease me because I was the smallest person in the class.

But I knew I was Chinese. One time when we went curling, these people were just amazed, making comments like, "Look, there's a Chinese girl curling — and there's another one!" We were such a shocking sight to them.

Another time I felt discriminated against was when I was applying for jobs after graduating from a business college course. I got through quite a few interviews, but I'd walk out of there knowing that I was not going to get the job. I just knew that they really wanted a beautiful white girl sitting in their office, not an Oriental.

ROBERTA

My feeling of not wanting to be Chinese started as far back as grade one. One time Mom sent me to school with my hair in braids. I was so embarrassed that I stayed outside of the school all morning. I never entered the building.

When I left home in my twenties I got to know myself and feel better about myself. Once you develop a bit more self-confidence, then you can accept yourself the way you are, instead of trying to be what you think others want you to be.

The biggest turning point was probably at college when I met the guy who later became my husband. Just before we got engaged, he took me to meet his family. He had warned me about their attitude.

Aside from racist name calling at school, I had never really encountered a great degree of racism before. So when I met my future mother-in-law, it was quite a blow when she said, "What do you think you're doing bringing *her* here!" But my husband stood behind me and said, "Well, if you don't like it, we won't come back again." It showed me that he really cared for me. He was willing to go against his parents' wishes. It was a decision he had to make — and he chose me.

Because we lost our ability to speak Chinese, we didn't have much to do with overseas Chinese. And we never knew any Canadian-born Chinese. But now I teach with a Chinese woman, and I've met a few others. When I was in high school I didn't want to be associated with any Chinese people. Now I've almost done a complete turnaround. I'm almost going out of my way to learn more about my own culture and try to get to know more Chinese people.

Before we went to school we all spoke Chinese fluently, but it faded because we were the only Chinese family and exposed to English most of the time. We spoke English at home to help Mom who was trying to learn English for working in the store. There wasn't any big push to keep Chinese traditions. But now I'm trying to learn Chinese again, maybe Mandarin. I'm taking a tai chi class. When I teach at school I usually try to introduce a unit on Chinese culture. I'm doing a lot of searching about my culture because I feel that I missed out on something.

I really do consider myself Chinese Canadian. I am still of

Chinese origin, even though I was brought up in the Canadian tradition. You can't change what you are.

JANET

I'm sure that most people who see me take it for granted that I'm an immigrant. I've gone into stores where people say to me, "Oh, are you one of those boat people?" When we were looking at houses, I'm sure that the real estate agent thought that he could push me around and get away with it because I was Oriental.

Since we've moved to Saskatoon, I haven't taken part in any of the festivities in the Chinese community, primarily because I don't know anybody. I suppose I could still go there, but I think, "Oh, I'll be the only one not being able to speak Chinese," so that inhibits me. I'd like to learn Chinese. I'd really like to.

ROBERTA

Well, Janet brought up a good point. I used to be like Janet, thinking, "I can't go because everybody will be speaking Chinese and I'll feel like I don't belong." But now, having spoken with one of the women from the Chinese Cultural Society, I feel like now I have a contact, someone I can work through to maybe become involved. So I'm definitely going to become involved in the next little while.

SHIRLEY CHAN

Shirley was born in Vancouver in 1947. She grew up in Chinatown and has been actively involved in community work, social planning and grassroots politics for many years. She and her parents spearheaded the organization of a tenants association in Chinatown which got the attention of the federal government. At the time of her interview, she was residing in Vancouver.

I always say that I was made in China, but born in Vancouver because my mother was six months pregnant when she arrived here. That was in 1947, the first year that the Chinese were allowed back in Canada after the Exclusion Act.

As a child, I had an awareness of being Chinese. I remember one day playing with my Scottish friend next door. I said that I was Chinese and she said, "Well, if you are, then I am." I said, "No, you're not." When I told her that she couldn't be, she got very upset and went home crying to her mother, who had to explain to her the fact that there were different races and cultures. This particular friend had not been raised to be conscious of race, but there were enough other people around who were racially conscious. And, as you know, the Chinese are as racist as any other group because they call whites "*gui lo*," meaning old ghost or devil. My parents made a choice to stay in the Chinatown area because they saw that it was important for us to learn the language and be exposed to the culture. From about the age of three until thirteen, my father spent time teaching me how to read and write Chinese. He was working, but he'd teach me in the morning before he went to work and at night when he came home. He would even assign us homework. When he wasn't teaching us Chinese, he was at the Lin-Chan Society, the *tong* — the family association. He was secretary-treasurer for years and years. Sometimes he would take us with him and we played ping-pong or watched television, since it was a long time before we had a television at home.

We had very few other recreational activities in our community, aside from the YWCA. I remember getting some brochures about summer camp from my teacher, but I threw them away before I got home because I didn't think my parents could afford to send me. I had a consciousness of the fact that we didn't have a lot of money. However, we always had shelter over our heads and food on the table. Those were the two things my parents worked very hard for. Mother worked in garment factories for as long as I can remember. She had two jobs to support the family.

Although I was the second born, I was always like the eldest. I have a sister, ten years older than me, who was born in China — but she didn't join us in Canada until she was fourteen. Then she got married when she was eighteen, so I didn't really know her. I used to call her *"hung san jie,"* which I interpreted as big sister from Red Mountain China,[1] and she would get very upset with me.

I spent a lot of time taking care of my sister who was three years younger. If I went out to play I had to let her tag along. I got the role of the big sister and the guilt that goes along with not having taken care of her properly. If she got hurt it was my fault since she was my responsibility.

Growing up near Chinatown where most of the people you see and go to school with are Chinese, you're a little sheltered. I guess some people would call it a "ghetto" — I'd call it a community with all the support networks…. One day, when I was very young, my mother asked another woman to pick me up from the local preschool. She forgot, so I had to wait and wait. Then I started walking home on my own. This truck driver who was delivering rice spotted me wandering on the streets. He put me in his truck and took me down to my father's store. If I had lived somewhere else, who knows what would've happened to me?

Most of the kids at my school were English as a Second Language students of Chinese origin. I loved my teachers and I wanted to be a teacher just like them. I especially remember my grade three teacher. She told us to write a story about a pilot. I wrote a little story about how girls weren't pilots — only boys could be pilots. So she asked to stay after school to discuss it. I told her that all the movies and books showed only men as pilots. This teacher said that girls could become anything they want to become. That was my first lesson in feminism. I'll never forget it.

There was no question in my parents' minds that a good education was important. Although my parents were considered working class because of their low incomes and immigrant status, they were well educated people with middle class, Chinese values. Even though I was a girl, my parents encouraged me to go to university. I know that some of my girl cousins did not have this kind of encouragement from their parents.

One year, I think I was in grade eleven, I got too wrapped up with dating to work very hard and I got a D in math, instead of my usual A or B. That freaked me out, so I dropped everything and started concentrating on my studies again.

Dating? Well, it's funny. I used to sneak out as much as anybody else. Because both my parents worked, I mostly went out with boys right after school. I remember whenever I went on a formal date I insisted on paying my own way, so I wouldn't feel obligated to anybody. I dated both Chinese and Caucasian guys when I was a teenager, and mainly those who had gone to the other elementary schools, rather than boys I had grown up with.

My parents certainly didn't approve of interracial dating. They talked about discrimination and language and cultural barriers. They would make comments like, "They may like you now, but in a few years they'll probably reject you. Look what happened to so-and-so who married *lo fan*. Now they're divorced and she's a single parent." I moved out for a while, just after high school and before university. I just needed the independence. Oh, I had a very strong will. My parents didn't like it, of course. No daughter should leave home until she gets married.

After two years at university, I moved to Toronto for a year. Then I came back to Vancouver in 1968 to continue school, but I got so involved in extracurricular activities, like my theatre group, that I didn't have much time for studying. Sometimes I'd work in the theatre until two or three a.m., and then crash in the costume room — then go to class at eight-thirty. I never asked my parents how they felt about all this, but I'm sure it drove them nuts. At the same time, many of my friends were moving into co-ops and getting involved with marijuana and mescaline and acid and stuff. It was a very hippyish era.

I didn't get into drugs or alcohol. I don't know why. Maybe it was because I grew up in a neighbourhood where I could see that people who abused alcohol ended up collapsing on the streets. I never saw the Chinese doing that. It was the *lo fan* and, unfortunately, native people too. I'd go to parties, but I never partook because I lack the enzyme that breaks down alcohol.

When I was in my third year of university, at the age of twenty-one, I attended a community meeting with my parents regarding an urban renewal plan that was going to happen. I listened to people from the city's social planning department explain how our Chinatown properties were going to be bought up by the city and torn down. The United Way also had a man there who was trying to help us relocate and prepare a brief to council to ask for fairer compensation. I listened to these Chinese people tell their stories through translators and I thought, "Gee, something should be done about this terrible situation."

At the meeting people were standing up and saying, "I put all my life savings in here" — or "This is my nest — we've worked hard to have a place to raise our family, to retire to and now you're going to take it all away from us" — or "Where are we going to move to when public housing is not suitable!" People who were approaching their retirement years, people who had spent all their lives working just to buy a place of their own, were now going to be forced to sell their homes to the city at an artificially depressed market value.

We began to organize a pretty strong lobby. My mother and I, along with some of the other neighbours, went door-to-door to ask people what they thought and whether they'd be interested in coming out and forming an association. We gathered signatures on a petition to try and collect money to hire a lawyer. My parents had saved up for a long time to buy their home. Then shortly thereafter, they heard about this urban renewal plan. The city said that only the old houses were going to be torn down, so my parents poured more money into upgrading the house. They put more and more money into it, believing that they would be saving their house from being torn down. But then we watched all our neighbours across the street move out. The place where their houses used to be became a playground for the new housing project. We watched the house which we once rented get torn down.

But public housing projects were a problem because of all the extended families in the Chinese community. Public housing only recognized small nuclear families — no space for grandmothers. The plan provided for a separate seniors' tower, but we didn't like that since it meant breaking up the family.

My mother did the door knocking. My father wrote newspaper articles and press releases, urging people to get up to protest this thing. We got the support of other people in the community who could articulate in English. We got people with political contacts. Nobody wanted to be chairman. My father, Walter Chan, was too sick, so he co-chaired with Sue Lum, a property owner, and Harry Con, a Chinatown businessman. The name of our association was the Strathcona Property Owners and Tenants Association (SPOTA), and we eventually managed to get the attention of the federal government.

Nothing would have happened if it weren't for my mother and her grassroots network of women factory workers and neighbours. She knew a lot of people. She was the one with boundless energy who would always volunteer to go door-to-door in any weather. She took a lot of abuse too. People would make comments like, "You're trying to get rich, going around collecting money door-to-door."

My experience with SPOTA, as a lobbyist at city hall and before the Federal Task Force on Housing, helped me develop a political consciousness. I was the one who helped appeal to the whole community with the message, "We're all hard-working people and we don't deserve to be thrown out." Prior to SPOTA, I was politically unconscious. I didn't pay attention to what was going on.

One of the other committees which grew out of SPOTA was the Association to Tackle Adverse Conditions (ATAC), a group of high school graduates who felt that we needed some decent recreational facilities in the area. Along with other people in the community, we put together the current Britannia Community Services Centre, a centre with a high school, library, elementary school, community centre, swimming pool and hockey rink.

When I graduated with a B.A. in English, I was offered a job with the Task Force on Citizen Participation. I went to Ottawa in 1971 on a three month research contract. From there I got other research contracts with citizen groups, and then the SPOTA people in Vancouver wanted me to come back. I got burned out because I lived in the area, right? I couldn't eat lunch or dinner without somebody coming by to see me, asking me to help them with a problem. I just worked too hard. And while all this was happening my father died.

It's a major impact when you lose a parent — someone whom you have loved and respected all your life. Although my father was very busy, I got to know him when I was in high school. Actually, when I was about sixteen, I'd been bugging my dad to let me have a driver's license because so many of my friends were driving. He kept refusing. I had given up and forgotten about it. Then one evening I came downstairs for a glass of milk before going to bed. He was still up, so I sat down and we started talking. We talked about politics and life and what it was like for him coming here. I started asking questions. Essentially, I started relating to him as a human being. We talked about society, culture, the world — and values. The next morning he said, "Well Shirley, I think you're ready for a driver's license." He took me completely by surprise. What was it that I had showed him? That I'd grown up? That I was a thinking adult, a responsible kind of person?

I didn't have time for marriage for a long time. After working for SPOTA, I worked for Health and Welfare in Ottawa for a while and spent too much time travelling. Oh, I thought about marriage off and on. I met a lot of different men. It wasn't hard to get a date. I threw away a few good opportunities to marry ... a few lawyers, some business people, other civil servants, some Chinese. I wasn't ready for it, I guess. Loss of freedom, loss of the right to make my own decisions — the fear of losing control over my life.

Some of these men were actually very fine people and I hurt a few along the way. It's unfortunate — not that I haven't been hurt too.

My poor parents were waiting for me to get married. They kept saying, "We'll stop worrying about you when you get married." Anyway, my mother was a matchmaker, but she never managed to match her own daughter. I always thought, "Gee, it would be nice to have a kid." I went through a struggle before hitting thirty. I thought, "Do I have a kid now, or do I forget about it? I could have it on my own. I could have artificial insemination." I wanted a child because there's a biological imperative to reproduce. This instinct to have a child is like hunger. If you ignore it long enough, it passes. But it comes back at different milestones in your life. Hitting thirty was one of those milestones. I decided then that I would not have a child on my own. I would need a strong support network for that. I knew that most of the men I knew wouldn't be able to provide me with the emotional support I needed for my career.

In 1975 I went to China during the Cultural Revolution and I fell in love with the people. They were so dedicated and caring, struggling to make a new society. They all had this goal to work towards a better society. They worked such long hours, six days a week. The guides and translators who travelled with us worked seven days a week. In 1978 I went to Japan, Hong Kong, Singapore and Taiwan with my mother, but these places were much more western than China was. In China I felt like I was in the Orient, in a different culture. Being in Japan was like being back in the Western world because of all the billboards and consumerism — the people pursuing careers rather than social goals.

As for careers and social goals, I always had a mixture of the two. My work has always been associated with trying to improve our community and society — to promote racial harmony or help people stand up for their rights. I remember some people telling me at the beginning not to rock the boat. But I grew up with my mother saying, "Don't forget what happened to the Japanese Canadians during World War Two. They all got interned and had their property taken away." Whenever I went out with Caucasians, she used to say that racism is still out there and it's not going to disappear. Racism here is not overt like it is in South Africa. It's insidious in our culture. You're supposed to be equal, but you really don't have equal opportunities if you're not white.

I think women have a really hard time too. You have to be twice as good. If I had been born a white, Anglo-Saxon male, I would have probably organized my life differently. I would have probably become an engineer or doctor and bought a house earlier, instead of "wasting time" working in community and social service projects. Men's careers are not threatened by marriage and having children. For a long time in our culture the belief was that a woman's primary job should be at home raising the children.

I didn't get married until 1983. Soon after that my kid was born. I finally met a man who could take on the primary parent role and permit me to focus on my career. My husband is Caucasian. He plays the piano as a ballet accompanist for many of the dance companies and dance schools in town, but I'm the major breadwinner. He looks after the baby. He's better at parenting than I am, very patient and creative. Sometimes it's hard to shake the socialization. Sometimes I think, gee, it would be nice to stay at home and be taken care of.

After I got my master's degree in Toronto in 1978, I went to work as a program co-ordinator for the Ontario Welfare Council, a job that brought me into contact with social planning councils across Ontario. Later I worked for Mike Harcourt, the mayor of Vancouver. When he got elected, he called to offer me this job because he had known me before. I had no doubts that it was the right move for me. I have a good understanding of communities and political process. I know how the federal government works and I have made a lot of contacts. Mike is good-natured and easy to work with. I just love my job.

I guess I'm more outspoken and aggressive than most Chinese women. Certainly putting my career first was something else that set me apart from them. My mother is like this too — an aggressive self-starter. She was a school teacher when women were not professionals. She learned to swim at the age of sixty-five, and that's not an easy thing to do. In some ways, she is much more fearless than I am.

Because my mother's first child was a girl, she wished that I had been a boy. I think that also had an impact on me. I had to prove that I was at least as good as a boy, if not better. I certainly had the example of a strong, hard-working, outgoing role model in my mother. In our own ways, we are both rebels.

When you're a workaholic, you sacrifice a lot of things like personal relationships, friends and family. It wasn't until my baby was born that I suddenly began to make family a priority. My son has given me a reason for why I want our society to be a better place. Now I have a son for whom I believe this world, whatever we leave of this world, is a legacy he inherits. So unless I strive to make this society a more caring, human place, I'd be doing him a disservice. He'll be living in the world of the future and there's so much room for improvement.

What do I want to do next? I really haven't come to grips with that yet. I feel that I should start looking for something else soon. I would like to broaden my experience once again and work in the private sector for a while. However, all my inclinations to working towards social equality say that I shouldn't be working for business, which is to work for profit. Also, it's natural when you work in government and community groups to think about politics as an option. We've got Bill Yee — the first Chinese Canadian alderman in Vancouver. We've got lots of women serving on council and in the House of Commons. But we still don't have any *Chinese* women. Maybe that's a goal I can try to aim for. I don't know. It's a big jump because being a politician is a very demanding life. You have to give up a lot. You have to be prepared to take a lot of crap. If it weren't for my son, I think I would have run in a couple of years time. Now I wonder if he's changed my values a bit, changed my priorities. But who knows? I might still do it.

Note

1. *hung san jie* — Shirley translates "hung san" as "red mountains." It should be noted that in Toisanese, the first part of this phrase is pronounced "hohng," a traditional reference to China.

SHARON LEE

Sharon was born in Port Alberni, B.C. in 1952 and moved to Vancouver as a teenager in 1967. She completed a degree in Fine Arts and later a degree in Nursing. Sharon has established herself as a visual artist and writer, publishing several works of fiction under the pen name, "Sky Lee" — short for "Sharon Kwan Ying Lee." She recently published the novel, Disappearing Moon Cafe.[1] At the time of her interview, she was residing in Vancouver.

When I was born my mother had already been in Canada for about two years. I was the fifth child and my parents were very, very poor, living in Port Alberni, a milltown in northern B.C. My father was working as a janitor in some scruffy, local hotels. He was born here and had grown up in Victoria.

Around 1936 he went back to China and married my mother. It was usual in those days for overseas Chinese to go back to China, get married and sire a son — as my father did. He returned to Canada for a while and then he went back to China again. This time he stayed for two or three years, which is when my older sister and another older brother were born. It wasn't until 1951 that my mother came to Canada with the children. They moved into Port Alberni because that was the only place where my father could find work.

Life in Canada was very isolating and alienating for my mother. Of course, when she came over here, she had baby after baby, and she was an older woman with failing health. Having to face the impersonal Western doctors with whom she couldn't communicate must have been very difficult for her.... Giving birth here was so different from her days in China, when her babies were delivered in her own bed with just a midwife beside her. She would have had lots of support from the community of women.

She told me this story once about one of her pregnancies. She had nausea and these certain cravings — one of them was fruit, right? Of course, back in China she was so used to eating all kinds of very nice vegetables and tropical fruits. When she came to Port Alberni, there was nothing. She had a craving for fruit, so finally my father went out one night for hours and hours. He left early evening and didn't come home until about eleven o'clock. He had gone up to Chinatown which was basically a community of overseas Chinese men with no families here. After some wheeling and dealing, all he could scrounge up was a couple of shrivelled up oranges for fifty cents. I mean fifty cents on their income would have been like ten or twenty dollars in our terms. So he brought these oranges home for my mother.

They were awfully poor. My mother couldn't even afford shoes. She told me stories of how she started her garden in March, digging away barefoot in the cold mud. My mother never attempted to Canadianize her thinking. She used to dry fish on our front yard and dry vegetables on our clothesline. Those were practical things, but she also kept superstitious traditions too — like we weren't allowed to wash our hair on special days.

Sometimes she'd go up to my elementary school football field to pick watercress. It was a private supply of watercress, apparently planted there many, many years ago by Chinese working in the mines. My mother would go out there with her little pail and start picking at the weeds to get at the watercress which was beside a ditch-like creek. My school friends would say, "Is that your mother? What are you guys eating? Finding weeds from the ditch or something?" I couldn't say, "What squatting Chinese woman? I don't see any Chinese woman squatting there. I don't know her." She was definitely my mother. Then on the other hand, I knew how delicious watercress was too, and if they didn't understand that — tough beans!

Port Alberni was a very racist community when I was growing up. There weren't many Chinese families. But I didn't really have an identity problem. We were so poor — so obviously from the wrong side of the tracks that there was no use wasting time feeling ashamed. Our family was just concerned about surviving. We children fully realized that our parents didn't have time to listen to us complain about things like having to eat steamed buns for lunch. We knew that if we didn't have steamed buns, we wouldn't have anything to eat. In a way, my brothers and sisters and I became fairly close because we were so alienated in this community with so few Chinese. So we learned basic survival techniques.

I had my own friends — friends from the other side of the tracks. Because I'm a very gregarious person, I didn't suffer too much at the hands of peer pressure. Even though I never got accepted by blonde girls in crinolines who had special little girl's bikes, I had my own tough neighbourhood group. We were the clique of poor ethnics — Italians, Japanese, East Indians. There were enough of us from the wrong side of the tracks that I didn't suffer too much from not being invited to parties.

I remember getting into real racial fights in junior high, being called a "Chink" or "Chinaman" — being all riled up with my fists all ready to go. I think these experiences toughened me. My parents never felt ashamed of themselves and they never let us feel ashamed. That really toughened us too. I mean there was such a polarized stance, no middle ground for us. I remember little episodes like there'd be a family of four boys that lived down the street, and my brother used to get into trouble with them. They'd call him "Chink" or "Chinaman." We became a family gang ourselves. We'd be out there with our sticks and my dad's leather belt, beating them and chasing them. They'd be chasing us too. Oh it was really kind of silly.

Things got better later on when my father was earning more money. He was able to buy a better car, a television — stuff like that. As I got older I noticed that I got invited to a certain number of birthday parties. As economic conditions in Port Alberni got better, so did race relations.

I remember that my father would encourage us in our private world within our home, but outside was a completely separate world where we had to fight and cope on our own. He'd encourage us to ham it up, singing and dancing or putting on skits. Pretending was like a form of self defense. But as soon as you got outside, you had to quieten down — to become invisible and non-threatening to whites. You had to be friendly on a superficial level, but not too friendly, in order not to get hurt. My father used to say, "Oh Sharon's so pretty. She's going to marry a doctor," and this and that, or "She's so smart. She's going to be a professor —

maybe even Prime Minister" — stupid comments like that. And yet when it came down to it, they never encouraged me to go to university. When I did go, they didn't help me financially at all. I think they could have contributed something, but they didn't. Another thing was that nobody said anything when I started getting As and Bs in grade five.

My parents didn't really participate in the community. As soon as we were out in school it was our world. It was very difficult because there were racist teachers too. I remember my sister's teachers would be calling her "Chinaman" — her *teachers*. One year I had to put up with a racist teacher who had failed my brother the previous year. She tried her best to level me too. In a way she succeeded, but it wasn't too bad. Now I know that there are nasty people in the world — and you have to stay away from them until you are emotionally prepared to fight them. They have various ways to intimidate and cripple you. You don't realize it until the injury is done.

When it comes to my son, Nathan, having to deal with racism, I wouldn't tag along to protect him. I wouldn't deal with individual incidences. Instead, I would work on building up his ego and build up the love in the family. It seemed to be enough for me. I realized that there was enough love in my family for me — and nothing can destroy that. However, it didn't seem to be enough for my brothers and sisters. They all have problems of one sort or another which I can directly attribute to poverty and racism. My parents did not consciously say, "Oh let's love, love our children and then they'll be strong." They were just as neurotic, and in many ways they were inept at dealing with racism. For instance, my father would get angry and frustrated at his work at the mill, but instead of identifying his real oppressors, he'd come home and oppress his family and destroy himself.

My parents' stubborn refusal to accept Canadian culture ironically boosted my identity. I think it's this middle ground that mixes kids up a lot — "Am I Chinese, am I Canadian, am I half and half?" Unlike other Chinese Canadians I met later in Vancouver, I never had that identity confusion and insecurity and guilt that I had to get over — I just went on, and on I went. I can't remember once when I wished I were white. Maybe I've suppressed that memory, I don't know. Racism hurt, but it didn't get me at the core.

In 1967 my parents decided to get us out of Port Alberni. They were afraid that I would get pregnant with a *lo fan* before the age of eighteen! So they moved the family to Vancouver and bought a house. I met all kinds of Chinese friends in Vancouver. This was good, but that was when I also developed a different sort of identity problem. I realized that none of my Hong Kong friends spoke Toisanese. In fact, they laughed at my accent, right? They're very class conscious, people from Hong Kong (laugh). I guess I shouldn't stereotype, but I found that they were prejudiced against Canadian-born — even more so than whites. That's why there's such a big rift between Canadian-born and new immigrants. Then I started meeting Chinese immigrant friends who were really hankering to become Canadianized. They naturally attached themselves to me because they perceived me as being very Canadian. Isn't that funny?

After taking "Chinese 100" at university, I went to China at the age of nineteen with three friends — a radical step in 1972 when there was next to no information available on China. That was probably when my biggest identity problem resolved itself. I realized that, hey, here are all these Hong Kong people trying to pass themselves off as being *real* Chinese, but they're no more Chinese than I am. In fact, their thinking is more colonialized than my thinking. The only *real* Chinese left in this world are the Chinese in China. Now I see my identity as definitely Canadian.

I did a degree in Fine Arts because I really wanted to become an artist, but I found it very discouraging. Male instructors wouldn't give me the time of day because I was a woman. Racist instructors wouldn't give me the time of day because I was not part of the WASP mainstream culture. People thought I was too young, or too poor — you know, just on and on. Eventually, I had to develop my own art, my own style. I discovered that what I had to say was more important than technique. So in a way, I became more of a political artist.

In fine arts courses it was like I was hitting blank walls all over the place. Finally I said, "Why am I allowing myself to be confused by these idiots who are telling me that art has to be WASP, and that you have to be a man or white to make it as an artist." I was really getting white-washed there. Finally it dawned on me, like wow, if I'm going to get down to the truth of art, I've got to have something to say, right? And I asked myself, "Do I have something to say?" And I thought, "Jeepers, I have lots to say." After that I did my first "Iron Chinks" series. Technically, it was just crappy — but what the hell, it had something to say.

"Iron Chinks" was actually the engraved name on a fish-cleaning machine. Chinese Canadian workers used to do really menial, hard labour in fish factories. I guess the capitalists tried to eliminate what little work the Chinese had by developing this automatic "Iron Chink" fish-cleaning machine, right? Chinese labour was reduced to the same level as a machine. It was really degrading. I used this title for my series because I saw all kinds of symbolism in it. But basically, my series was portraits of my family, combined with writing about my experiences growing up. That was the first time people had valid comments to make about my work. So I realized that I had finally found what I wanted to do.

Being a so-called politically conscious artist, I decided that I needed to get into printing. I wanted my art to reach a mass audience, and that means publication and printing, right? So off I went down Commercial Street into the first printing shop I saw, and I said, "I want to know about printing. Are you willing to give me a job?" And the guy said, "Hey! You know there's a women's art collective across the street." So I went across the street to *Makara*, and that's where I finally learned confidence in myself as a woman and as an artist. I worked there with these other women for over a year and really got my shit together (laugh). I guess I must have had some talent because they kept on encouraging me. They were women like me who had encountered the same racism, the same class conscious elitism.

If I had something to say, it had to be said. Another good way to get it across was with words on paper, right? So I started writing too. I actually had the first story I wrote published. I thought that was really strange, so I wrote another story which also got published.

My pen name is Sky Lee. It's my actual name, not a pseudonym — Sharon Kwan Ying Lee — my initials. I remember this funny editor who called and asked to speak to Sky Lee. When I replied that I was Sky Lee, she said, "God, are you a *woman*? I thought you were a man!" I found that interesting, but I've had a couple of comments like that, actually.

When I was younger I had no idea that I was going to write because I always thought I was a crummy writer. But I discovered that you have to forget all the phony standards. If you've got something relevant to say, say it. I don't care if it comes out in schizophrenic poetry. You can write it as graffiti on the walls.

I want all of our community art and writing to become part of mainstream culture. But we shouldn't have to *goy* (change). Canadian attitudes should change. I have this theory — I suddenly realized that "Canadian" is not just hockey and apple pie. It means all kinds of things — anything from any immigrant, new or old — because we're all immigrants here. None of us have been in Canada long enough to set cultural standards for other people. Canadian is anything from roti to red New Year's packets. So the next new immigrant who squats down on his thongs to eat salted fish and rice with chopsticks is just as Canadian as a RCMP guy on a brown horse. Therefore, what we Chinese Canadians find out in our identity seeking work is just as relevant to a … Yugoslav Canadian. We've all been sucked in by these colonial in-group versus out-group values. My efforts in seeking Chinese Canadian identity is more Canadian than hockey, more Canadian than … I don't know, the Vancouver Symphony Orchestra! (laugh)

I'm no role model for other young Chinese or Asian Canadians because nobody comes specifically from my background — and nobody has quite my ego (laugh). I would certainly hope that if they see something about me that they're interested in, they would come up and get to know me because I'm very talkative. I'll talk to anybody. The trouble is most people probably think I'm a bit eccentric, but that's all right.

I got into nursing because I needed a good, honest job right away. I could have gone into social work, but I didn't perceive it as a very honest, true to life type profession. I wanted something practical, basic blood and guts. Nursing is like that. You go into work and you see a patient who's in pain, but you know how to deal with that pain in a very practical way. I love nursing. It's a great job. But you can't let yourself get emotionally involved — that's not to say that I don't get emotionally involved sometimes, because I do. If you want melodrama, go to the hospital.

I feel grounded now. Parenting has grounded me. If you're going to have a child — if you're going to nurture another human being, you have to become a full human being yourself. You have to come to terms with your philosophies of life and death. Raising a human being is not just having the ability to change a diaper. You have to raise a human being with a true blue heart.

Note

1. Sky Lee. *Disappearing Moon Cafe* (Vancouver: Douglas MacIntyre, 1991).

PHOTOGRAPHS

Haw Chow Shee with son George and infant daughter, Avis Haw
— the first Chinese Canadians born east of the Rockies (1897).
(*Professor Douglas H. Lee Collection*).

Margaret Chan (1902–1989). One of the first Chinese women to go through the public school system in Victoria, B.C.
(Margaret Ko Collection)

Mrs. Lee Sing Wei entered Vancouver in 1919. She paid $500 Head Tax. *(Lee King Family Collection)*

Chinese Canadian Women's Auxiliary in the 1910s.
(British Columbia Archives)

Graduating class, Victoria Chinese Public School, 1920s.
(Margaret Ko Collection)

Dr. Victoria Cheung. The first woman graduated from the University of Toronto Medical School, 1923.
(Margaret Ko Collection)

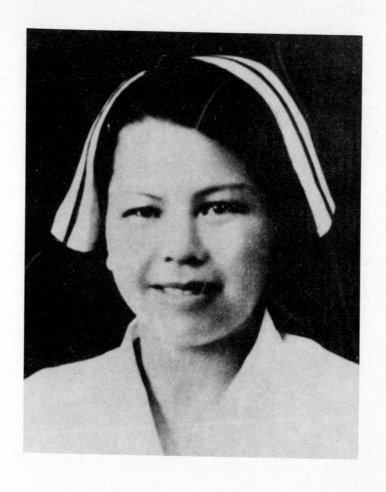

Agnes Chan (1923). The first Chinese nurse to graduate from Toronto Women's College Hospital, School of Nursing.
(Margaret Ko Collection)

March in Victoria, B.C. 1933. *(Susie Nipp Collection)*

Women's group in Chinese Presbyterian Church, Toronto.
(Daniel Mah Collection)

Women in a race, Chinese School picnic, Elk Lake, Victoria, B.C. 1935. *(Susie Nipp Collection)*

THE WOMAN'S PART IN WAR

KNITTING FOR CANADIANS in uniform is the task of these four members of the Chinese church, Elm and Bay Sts., Toronto. They have been turning out sweaters and socks for some time Formerly they knitted for Chinese troops. Left to right, Mesdames Mark Shung, Chin Tank, Kan Ko, Ing Look

"The Woman's Part in War." *(Valerie Mah Collection)*

Mary Ko Bong with brother John, two of four of Ko Bong family who served in Second World War. (*Mary Ko Bong Collection*)

Fern and mother, brothers, and sisters. 1961.
(Fern Hum Collection).

Women's Group, Sudbury. Knox Presbyterian Church, 1950.
(Fern Hum Collection)

Mary Mohammed married to Dr. Auyuab. 1955.
(*Mary Mohammed Collection*)

Jean Lumb with Prime Minister Diefenbaker and Foon Sien Wong and cross Canada delegates to present the brief on the Appeal of Immigration Changes, 1957. *(Jean Lumb Collection)*

Valerie Mah with seniors at the Toronto Mon Sheong Home for the Aged. 1985. *(Valerie Mah Collection)*

Winnie Ng teaching English as a Second Language in a garment factory, 1986. *(Winnie Ng Collection)*

Tam Goosen with a class at Withrow Public School, Toronto. 1992. *(Tam Goosen Collection)*

THEMES

COMING TO GUM SAN

JEAN LEE

Jean was born in Windsor, Ontario in 1919. At the time of her interview, she was still residing in Windsor.

My father came to Canada around 1905. He worked his way over on a ship as a cook. Then he got a job as a houseboy. While he was in Victoria, he heard that there was more freedom if he moved inland because he'd be able to own property and start his own business.[1] So he came to Windsor and opened The Savoy, the first Chinese restaurant in Windsor. He saved his money and got my mother, my brother and a nephew over. It cost him $1,500 Head Tax to bring them here, $500 each.... My father was very frugal. He allowed himself only one cigar a week, so that he could save the money to bring his family over.

My mother arrived in 1918. They kept her, like everyone else from China, in quarantine for a month in Vancouver. Then she came to Windsor. She never said much about it. She said that it was like being in jail for a month. I guess it was pretty hard and lonely because they didn't understand the language. My mother learned a little bit of English, picking it up as she went along, but she didn't become fluent in it.

SALLY WONG

Sally was born in Hong Kong in 1962. She immigrated to Canada in 1968. At the time of her interview, she was residing in Edmonton.

I loved it in Toronto. The first thing I saw when I looked out the window was a squirrel in a big, big maple tree. And then there were sparrows chirping on the trees. It was so peaceful and quiet. That was my first impression of Canada. All I wanted to do was go out and play.

And just down the street was Riverdale Zoo. So whenever we didn't have school, we'd go down there and collect pop bottles. You'd get two cents back for each bottle at the corner store. Our cousins had come to Toronto first and they took us around. They taught us what to do to get money.

MAY CHOW

May was born in China in 1937. She immigrated to Canada in 1953. At the time of her interview, she was residing in Kamloops, B.C. The following excerpt from her story was translated from Cantonese.

I was born in Toisan, China. My father came to Canada in 1920 because my uncle had a wholesale produce business here. Those days, you could sponsor people to come here as workers. My father had to pay the $500 Head Tax. He went back to China in 1935. I was born in 1937. Three months later, he returned to Canada alone because of the immigration restrictions at that time. The rest of the family came here in 1953. In the years in between he didn't visit us — didn't even send money. I think, maybe, Canada had laws from 1938 to prohibit people from sending any money home. So for eight years we never got any money. My mother had to sell clothes and things from the house. Life was difficult in the 1930s. When my father began to send us money again, I went to school immediately. I was already nine.

Before coming to Canada, I stayed in Hong Kong for several months. The Canadian immigration office there asked me many questions: "Where is your home? Which room did you eat in? Which room did you sleep in?" They were afraid that some children were not the real children of the sponsor. In those days people sometimes had to use documents belonging to others. My father could have sold my document for $1,600 Canadian. Therefore, it was very special that I was able to come — that he did not sell my document. Everybody said that he was stupid, that he didn't know how to make money. Other people sold their daughters' documents because girls could get married and have their husbands sponsor them, instead of their parents.

Each day in Hong Kong I had to recite my testimony: my age, my mother's age, the location of my village, how far it is from Hong Kong, from Guangzhou, my father's occupation.... My mother had to recite this information too. They approved me, but not my mother. They claimed that there was something wrong with her lungs, so she had to stay in Hong Kong for another two years.

MAY CHEUNG

May was born in Guangdong, China in 1935. She immigrated to Canada in 1956. At the time of her interview, she was residing in Toronto. The following excerpt has been translated from Cantonese.

When I first came to Vancouver, Salt Water City, in December, 1956, I was so scared by the snow. I wondered how I would be able to walk in it. When we were on the train to Toronto, all I could see was snow. I stayed home all the time. I didn't even go out once a month. Even if I wanted to go out, how could I? There were no Chinese. We lived in the High Park area. We lived on the third floor of my husband's brother's house. Later in 1962 when we already had four children, we got together some money and bought a house. It took us a long time to save up the money. My husband only earned $60 a week, working from eight in the morning until midnight, or sometimes even three in the morning.

MYRTLE WONG

Myrtle was born in Bendigo, Australia in 1922. She immigrated to Canada from Australia in 1946 as a war bride. At the time of her interview, she was residing in London, Ontario.

I came to Canada from Australia in 1946. I lived in the home of a Canadian who had looked after my husband from the time he was nineteen years old. This man was a highly respected Queen's Council lawyer. On the days when the maid was not in, I helped with the laundry and cooking. I was not glad to be here at first because I missed my family and I had to face a lot of racism from people who mistook me for a Japanese. When I arrived in London, Ontario, nobody knew me. I wasn't very well accepted. I'd walk into a store and people would slam the door in my face, thinking I was Japanese. In Australia my whole family was well known and respected, but here I was just like an ant. So that was an adjustment. It was like I fell off the ladder.

But there was one very kind family nearby who made me feel welcome and helped me bridge the gap. If I had to go anywhere, they would accompany me so I wouldn't get lost. They got me accustomed to the Canadian way of doing things: the right clothing, food, transportation, holidays. The mother of this family treated me like a daughter. This family really made it easy for me. I was already fluent in English, so I adapted very quickly.

We didn't keep Chinese customs. Remember, my husband did not recognize any Chinese tradition, so it was pointless for me to adhere to my Chinese upbringing. My friends were Caucasian, so I just went their way. You know the saying, "When in Rome, do as the Romans do"? That's exactly what I did.

MAY MAH

May was born in Hong Kong in 1933. She immigrated to Canada in 1953. At the time of her interview, she was residing in Calgary, Alberta. The following excerpt has been translated from Cantonese.

I came in November, 1953. I met my husband in Hong Kong. He had come here a year earlier, but there was no way for me to come then, so my father-in-law had to buy me a "paper," a birth certificate from another family. My father-in-law had been in Canada for sixty years already, and he had sponsored my husband to come. Back then it was very difficult to find "papers" for women because most people had "papers" for men, which could be sold at a higher price. I heard that even if people gave birth to daughters, they still reported that they gave birth to sons, just so that they could sell the birth certificates at a higher price.

The price of my paper was quite reasonable, only $1,500 Canadian — compared with the papers for men, $100 Canadian for each year of age. Yes, the immigration policy was relaxed by 1953, but since my father was not Canadian, I would not be able to come. And the government would still not allow men to bring over their fiancées.

My father-in-law had two wives. My husband's mother is the first wife. His father thought that his first family had died in the Second World War because he had lost contact with them for seven or eight years, so he remarried. Actually, his first family was still alive. When he found that out, he sponsored them to come, one by one. After our arrival, we did not get along very well with his second wife. A complicated family naturally generates arguments. And my father-in-law could not care less, listening only to the younger wife.

Before I got here, I thought Canada would be slightly better than Hong Kong. Hong Kong is a small place with so many people. The living environment is not that good. So I thought that life in Canada could not possibly be less comfortable. My first impression was of the extreme cold. It was still very warm in Hong Kong when I left there, but in Calgary it was thirty-six below. None of my clothes or shoes suited the weather here. I had never expected it to be this cold. My husband had to buy me some winter clothes at The Bay department store.

I missed my family very much. They were all in Hong Kong. I did not have a single relative here. I cried almost every night, but I never seriously thought about going back to Hong Kong. Adding to my loneliness was the fact that I did not speak English. I wanted to take the citizenship class. But I got pregnant shortly after my marriage because I didn't know about contraceptive methods. So I never got a chance to go to school in Canada.

I missed my family even more after my father died in 1958. I was sending them about $100 a month. If I hadn't done so, they could not have supported themselves. My whole family, except my eldest brother, finally came here by 1968. I had to buy a "paper" for my younger brother who was eleven at the time. It cost $2,100, including commission. No matter how poor I was, I wanted to reunite my entire family. I wanted my brothers and sisters to survive. How could they have survived in Hong Kong by merely depending on my mother? I knew that their lives would be better here. As the eldest sister, it was my responsibility to bring my younger siblings over here. As the old saying goes, "Sacrifice the smaller self and fulfill the greater self."

SHIRLEY WELSH

Shirley was born in China in 1949. She immigrated to Canada in 1954. At the time of her interview, she was residing in Edmonton.

I was already seven years old when I started grade one because I missed the September term. Then, because of my poor English, I failed grade one. That set me back two years. But I managed to learn English quickly and after that I was sailing. I was in Swift Current, Saskatchewan. We had come from Hong Kong by an oceanliner to San Francisco. We took the train from San Francisco to Whiterock, B.C., and then we took another train from there to Swift Current.

I remember that it was snowing when we got off the train. That was quite an experience because we had never experienced snow before in Hong Kong. Compared with Hong Kong, there was so much space in Saskatchewan — and there were lots of white people (laugh).

I was fascinated. At that young age, I remember so vividly the differences between Hong Kong and Canada. For example, back home we had to do a lot of repetition in school, reading aloud in unison. But here the teaching methods were more spontaneous. I adapted very, very quickly to the Canadian ways.

TAM GOOSEN

Tam was born in 1947. She immigrated to Canada in 1970. She now lives in Toronto.

When I was in Hong Kong, I felt a bit out of place because a lot of people were only interested in making money while my friends and I were more interested in foreign films. I always thought that once there's a chance, I'd like to leave Hong Kong. I had always been fascinated by North American Chinese since none of my family had ever gone overseas. My first choice was the United States where Ted was. We had met in Hong Kong in 1969 on his way home from studying in Japan. He was the catalyst that finally made me work out my plan to leave Hong Kong. I couldn't get a visa for the States, so I came to Canada. I had heard that the Canadian consulate was still taking applicants for immigration and the whole process took half a year. I found out that I could use my secretarial skills, otherwise I probably wouldn't have been accepted as a single woman. My family was very much behind me, but my mother was still frightened. God knows, they had no idea what was going to happen to me!

RAMONA MAR

Ramona was born in Fort Smith, Northwest Territories in 1957. She now resides in Vancouver.

My paternal grandfather came to Vancouver as a young man of twenty-one in 1911. After a few years he took the *Blue Funnel* line back to China to marry the woman whom my great-grandmother had chosen for him to marry. He wanted to bring her back, but the Canadian Exclusion Act was in force. He managed to wrangle her into this country, telling the officials that he was a businessman, hence, entitled to bring his wife over. He had set up a shoe repair shop at that time. He became quite successful. He also did well at buying and selling Chinatown properties. He was one of the first Chinese Canadians to buy a huge mansion in the posh Shaughnessey areas of Vancouver. At first they didn't want to sell to Chinese Canadians. They wanted to keep it an exclusively white district. It was blatant discrimination. He bought the property after they opened it up in the 1930s and 1940s. If there was one thing my grandfather could do, it was work hard and save money.

MAE LEE

Mae was born in Union Bay, B.C. in 1915. At the time of her interview, she was residing in Victoria, B.C.

I think my mother was able to get into Canada because my grandfather and father were probably among the first Chinese Canadians with naturalization papers. My grandfather worked for this Canadian named James Dunsmuir. He was a big wheel who owned all these coalmines up in Cumberland. He might have had something to do with getting my mother over here. When my grandfather died after returning to his village in China, my father took over what he had left in Canada. My father always had this picture of Mr. Dunsmuir in his office. We were supposed to remember how he's such a good man to help us — this white-haired fellow, very nice looking, old, old man.

When my mother was in China, she had bound feet, but when she came over here she took off the cloth. Her feet were so small and funny looking. She could hardly walk. It was very painful. Mother was very lonely at first. The houses were so far apart, compared with houses in China. Then of course, after she had lived in Union Bay for quite some time, she didn't mind.

SHIN MEI LIN

Shin Mei was born in Indonesia in 1936. She immigrated to Canada from Taiwan in 1965. At the time of her interview, she was residing in Halifax, Nova Scotia. The following excerpt from her story has been translated from Mandarin.

I was studying nursing in Taiwan when I met my husband. Three years later we got married and he set up his own clinic. But he wanted to become better qualified, so he came to Halifax in July, 1965. Four months later, I joined him with our two children.

My first impression of Halifax was that it was desolate. It was a Saturday when we arrived and there were no people on the streets! It was horrifying. The room we rented was very small and the rent was $300! The only time I went out was to go to the store to buy food. I was so bored. My husband was always busy at the hospital. He even had to be on duty on weekends. The children and I spent a lot of our time watching TV.

The worst years in Canada for me have been these two years after my husband died during heart surgery in Montreal.... When I first came to this country, everything was so different — the lifestyle, food — but difficulties went away so quickly ... because as long as you're with your family, whatever kind of suffering seems to be endurable.

GRACE LEE

Grace was born in Victoria, B.C. in 1902. She went to China with her family in 1911. Then in 1928 she returned to Canada. At the time of her interview, she was residing in Victoria. This excerpt has been translated from Cantonese.

I chose to come to Canada because I wanted to be a teacher and the pay was much higher here. Also, I wanted to feel independent. I was born in Canada and returned to China at the age of nine, so I thought why not return to Canada to teach. However, soon after my arrival, I wanted to go back to China. I was so desolate when I first came.

I couldn't bear the differences between the two countries. For example, I tried to teach Chinese to the students here the same way I did in China, but the students and their parents didn't understand what I was trying to do. I had to change my whole way of life. Wardrobe was another problem. I felt very insulted by rumours that they thought I was a servant in a restaurant because of the way I dressed. So I had western style clothes made, instead of wearing the *cheong sams*, the traditional Chinese dresses I had brought with me.

Note

1. British Columbia passed legislation at the municipal and provincial levels that made it virtually impossible for Chinese to own land.

OUR MOTHERS
AND FATHERS

RAMONA MAR

My mother was the fifth of ten kids. There was a string of eight girls — and then two boys. It was implicit that my grandfather really wanted boys. He was extremely strict and authoritarian. My mom was the first out of her family to choose her own spouse. She had seen her older sisters matched up and realized she didn't want that for herself. She was born in Vancouver and was quite westernized. She met my father, the bush pilot, and he whisked her off to Sioux Lookout in Ontario. It worked out quite well. When I was in grade one, the whole family moved to Vancouver. Then a year later my father was transferred to Prince Rupert, and the following year he died in a plane crash. I was only ten and my sisters were eight and six…. My mother was still quite young.

The night of the crash, Mother came up to our bedrooms. Tucking in each one of us, she said, "Don't worry, if anything ever happens, I'll be your mommy and daddy." I remember that so clearly. It made me feel secure and safe. The next day we went to school since we didn't know the seriousness of the crash yet. A search team had been dispatched. I remember hearing a radio report while we were waiting for a friend: "Hong Mar, a bush pilot of Prince Rupert, is missing in an air accident. Search teams are looking…" and I remember thinking, "That's my dad." They found the wreckage that night. He'd crashed on a mountainside.

This tragedy really made our family close. All of a sudden, we weren't mother and father and three kids. We were four young women living together. And because I was the eldest, I became sort of my mother's spouse in a lot of ways. She would talk to me about adult things, and I think that made me grow up a lot faster.

Mother moved us back to Vancouver — to our grandfather's house. She returned to a map-making store where she had worked before. The people who owned the store remembered her from when she was a young girl and were quite sympathetic. This job, drafting maps, started out part-time at first, since that's all she wanted to do. While she was at work, our grandmother would watch over us. It worked out quite well. We certainly enjoyed being around our aunts, uncles and cousins. It was a happy time.

The four of us slept in one room, even though the house was so huge. Our room had two double beds, and my two sisters and I would take turns sleeping in Mom's bed each night. We were paranoid that she would leave us, or be taken away like our father was, so that we'd be orphaned and separated. You know, if she was five minutes late, we'd go meet her at the bus stop — and if her bus was late, we'd worry. This paranoia lasted about three years, but it still comes to the surface sometimes. Because my mother is my only parent, she's that much more precious to me. I'm so afraid of losing her, even though she's perfectly healthy and can look after herself.

Oh, my mother was strict with us but in a different way. She was born here, so she's got a little of both cultures. She wanted to give us freedom within a boundary. I remember she'd take us to restaurants to teach us table manners and the concept of "eating out." We also had an aunt who took us to plays and movies. We went on family picnics — and of course, birthdays were a big deal. My mom went out of her way to make a big deal of things for us.

By the time we were all in school, my mother was working full-time. She really takes pride in her independence.... When I was in university, I brought home Betty Friedan's *Feminine Mystique*, and I told my mother to read it. She enjoyed it and we talked about it. I think Betty Friedan said the things my mother had always believed. She just hadn't heard anyone say these things so articulately before.

VELMA CHAN

Velma was born in Merritt, B.C. in 1908. At the time of her interview, she was residing in Vancouver.

My mother was brought over to Canada by a family when she was a young girl. At about eighteen years old, she married my father who was about twenty years her senior. They didn't choose each other. The mistress of the family that brought her over chose my dad for her.

I had a close relationship with my mother. She was very understanding. She knew that girls had to have a life of their own, but she was bound by custom as well. When she had time, she talked to me about the old ways. What a proper girl has to do (laugh). For instance, you weren't supposed to talk. You had to pull your weight and look after the younger ones. Outside of that, she didn't talk to me much. And my father was very, very strict. He was a man of the old school. Although he did realize that to get along in Canada, you had to have an education.

Mother always tried to maintain a routine where we could have time to do our homework. After school we'd do the necessary chores, like bringing in some wood and getting things ready for supper, but right after supper she'd do the dishes which *we* were supposed to do. She'd do them, so we could go off and do our homework.

We tried to follow the teachings of our mother. We didn't know better. It was a proper upbringing in those days. We didn't mix too much with Caucasians because we were more or less excluded. We lived far away. Our clothes were different. Our manners were different. My mother used to make homemade garments for us, and they weren't fashionable. She'd order from the Eaton's catalogue — and to get a good bargain, she used to buy things bigger and longer than what we needed, so we could get full use out of them.

VALERIE MAH

Valerie was born in Brockville, Ontario in 1940. She currently resides in Toronto.

I used to have eczema as a child. I remember my mother used to go to the poultry place and get chicken feathers. She'd boil them to make a solution. I used to have to wash in it. It's an old Chinese remedy for getting rid of the itch or something. It was very smelly.

My mother was declared "Citizen of the Year" in Brockville

once. She was the kind of person who worked in the restaurant, raised five kids, but still found time to be head of the Boy Scout Women's Auxiliary. She isn't a typical Chinese female. She raised us as Canadians. I admire my mother. She's worked hard all her life, and I think she likes doing what she does, which is to be with people and run a restaurant. But she's seventy-five. I wish I could go and help her now, but I have my life in Toronto. So I'm in a bit of a dilemma. I can't visualize her in an old age home because she's too damn independent. But maybe if she was in a home we'd be doing some of the internal organizing, so she'd be the stimulus for the residents to become more involved in some of their own programming....

My mother's grade twelve education at the beginning of the century would have been the influence of the church in North Bay, I guess. They pushed the idea that she should go to school. My husband Daniel's mother was even more unique. She came over in 1914 as a picture bride. Her husband had gone back to China and had about forty pictures of young girls to choose from, all lined up by the matchmaker. She used to teach Bible studies to other women in the community. Both my mother and my mother-in-law were very unusual women.

My father felt very inadequate sometimes because he only had a grade eight education. But we said that he shouldn't put himself down, because he managed to build up three restaurants and get shares in other restaurants. He was a very outgoing person. My mother was very quiet, but then after my dad died, running the business on her own, she became more independent and outgoing, out of necessity. There had been a certain amount of dominance by him.

I remember doing things with my dad a lot. I was quite close to him. I used to go to wrestling matches with him. You know when they cheated, I'd be yelling, "Cheating! Cheating! Look at that! Look at that!" I also used to go fishing with my dad. My older sister used to go duck hunting with him. We had a cottage five miles up the river. We'd closed the restaurant on a Wednesday afternoon and go off fishing. We went on family holidays, but somebody always had to stay home and look after the restaurant, seven days a week.

My father was quite well respected in the community. After he closed down the restaurant at night, he'd go over to the police station and sit and chat with the guys over there. If they had calls, he'd go with them in the police car. I mean, small town. He spoke very good English. He was very friendly. Everybody liked him.

I remember one night when I was in high school. I was walking down the street on Hallowe'en night, and a police car went by. I said to my girlfriend, "Huh! They're probably out looking for me." And the police car turned around and the officer said, "Hey Val, your dad's looking for you." So you couldn't do anything wrong in a small town because everybody knew you, and everybody would, you know, squeal on you to your parents. But there was nothing wrong with living that way.

We all had chores to do. My dad did the buying and he worked in the kitchen. Mother was out front, but Dad was out front sometimes too. Dad was a good cook. I can remember having venison, steak, scallops and lobster. Mom wasn't as good a cook as Dad.

LINDA LEE

Linda was born in Halifax, Nova Scotia in 1950. At the time of her interview, she was still residing there.

My mother lived very much what I would have considered a traditional Chinese woman's life in Canada. While my father was alive, he took care of anything that needed taking care of outside of the house. Mom was comfortable enough with English to do grocery shopping, for example, to use the bus lines, to go to the shops in the neighbourhood where people knew her but not much more than that. Her life was centred around my father and the children and her Chinese friends.

Mom also had some very good Canadian friends. We became very close to a Dutch-Austrian family who boarded in our house when they first arrived. Mrs. Krause spoke German and my mother spoke Chinese, but they became very close friends. They would talk about family or past history. They had shared so many experiences that they always understood each other.

Mom used to talk about her first Christmas here. She would have arrived August or September, and the other members of the Chinese community told her what people in Canada did for Christmas — that they would cut down a tree and bring it inside the house and decorate it with lights and things. My mother said she was sure for the longest time that they were all pulling her leg. She couldn't imagine that you would bring a tree into the house (laugh).

My mother once recounted her experience of going to the hospital to have my sister, May. Now this would only have been a couple of months after she arrived in Canada. She didn't speak English at all. And she had never been in a hospital — to have a child or anything else. My father couldn't stay with her since men didn't accompany women into the delivery room in those days. Mom was surrounded by people she didn't know, who didn't speak her language — and she was just terrified when she saw the tray of surgical instruments go by. Years later she just laughed about it, but we thought it must have been a terrible experience for her.

We used to tease my mother about where children came from. She was never comfortable talking about anything like that. I can remember us sitting around the dinner table and saying, "Oh, come on..."

Mom was still maintaining, in the face of three teenagers who had all taken biology, that we had come from Citadel Hill, a landmark here in Halifax. She told us that nuns from the Halifax Infirmary had gone to the Hill and gotten us there and brought us back to her at the hospital. And I'm sure she knew that we knew she was lying because we were all laughing and she was very pink. But no, she wasn't going to change the story that she had give us all those many years (laugh).

SALLY WONG

I was just so depressed and I couldn't concentrate when we were having problems at home. I started skipping classes. And I went on a diet. I went down to eighty something pounds — and then suddenly my weight shot up to about one hundred and thirty pounds. Anyway, in January when we were skipping school, a teacher called home and asked where we were. My parents *hate* any kind of trouble. When I got home that night around midnight, Dad called me to the kitchen and we had a showdown. He said, "If you don't want to go to school, you can quit and go to work — or else you go to school and you quit your job and come home right at three-fifteen!" So, I left. My sister came with me. This time when he kicked us out, we knew it was coming.

LIL LEE

Lil was born in Nanaimo, B.C. in 1927. At the time of her interview, she was residing in Vancouver.

I had two older brothers and an older sister. My older sister, she passed away, so I became very close to my mother. Mother is a very soft woman. I cannot remember her ever really being angry. So we grew up in quite a good environment, under her care. Well my dad was very strict, but he didn't do that much disciplining. I think it was really my mother who taught us more — how to behave and what we should do and what we shouldn't do. She taught us just the same old things that most mother teach their daughters — to be good and not to be loose, things like that.

My parents didn't allow us to do a lot of things. The boys were freer. They could stay out later at night while we girls couldn't go to dances and parties. The girls were just supposed to stay home and learn how to cook and sew and behave well — and wait for the time to get married (laugh).

FRANCIS WONG

Francis was born in Brantford, Ontario in 1921. At the time of her interview, she was residing in London, Ontario.

My mother always preferred the boys — yes, definitely. She always made sure that they were looked after. But the girls, we didn't matter since we get married off. That's the Chinese tradition.

My mother couldn't speak English at all. Just broken English — and she was laughed at. They'd make faces and call you all kinds of names. Some customers came into our restaurant and would walk out because she wasn't able to speak to them. Some were very ignorant. Adults even. They'd come in, put their fingers up to their eyes and pull them out. I guess that made her angry, so she didn't want us to associate with the Canadians.

DR. LINDA LEE

Linda was born in Toronto in 1953. At the time of her interview, she was residing in Saskatoon, Saskatchewan.

Both my parents are dead now. My mother came here in 1919. She said that her mother had too many kids, so she sold her to a woman who was coming to Montreal. She was her maid, but I guess they told customs that she was a niece. Mother worked in Montreal for this lady until she was sixteen. She never went to school — never learned to read or write.... I don't know when my father came. He was very old. He died in 1967, at the age of eighty-four. I don't know where he was from. He married my mother about 1925 — when she was only sixteen and he was forty-four! We don't know how old she was exactly. She lied on her passport and went by the Chinese calendar. So whenever it was convenient for her to have a birthday, or to be a certain age, she was. My father had another family in China though ... somewhere.

I remember my mother saying that when she first came to Canada, she used to peek through keyholes in this big, old Montreal house and see people smoking opium. She said she would watch them — in the house of the woman she worked for.... I think she was very bitter about being sold at the age of nine or ten. She never got a chance to go to school. I mean, the woman bought her to work as a maid, cooking and cleaning. I know that my mother didn't really like my father very much. There were some younger guys she was more interested in, but my father had more money, so she had to go with him. That's all she ever said about it. She didn't even know how my father had paid for her.

There were nine of us children and, well, my mother used to beat us all up for no good reason. I think she was just very frustrated, beating whomever was there at the time. But I remember the Children's Aid Society coming by because the teachers used to complain that we'd come to school with bruises. And we'd have to lie, saying, "Oh well, I fell down" — or "I walked into the door." The teachers would report it, but they couldn't do anything about it. We lied because she was standing right there! Oh, she could speak English. I think she just picked it up on her own.

My father didn't speak English, but he understood it. He would speak to us in Chinese, and we'd answer him in English, but we'd both understand. I remember how my father used to look after us. He used to pick us up from school. He did all the cooking. He used to work in the garden all the time. He'd try to protect us, try to stop my mother from beating us, but I guess he was pretty old. He could yell at her, but my mother had more power in the family. I don't remember him having any power. My sisters and I haven't really talked about this a lot, but I think my father really loved my mother. However, she couldn't stand him. I think he tried to please her. We were very poor, yet he'd go and buy her things when we didn't have any food. He always seemed to be trying to get her approval, and she didn't want to have anything to do with him.

Later I became close to my mother. She had had a stroke and was pretty much housebound. There were only three of us left at home at the time, and I guess I used to look after her more than the others did (sigh). I was probably more docile. She used to fight with the other two all the time while I was the referee. But then she just mellowed so much. She just wasn't so much of a fighter anymore.

My mother used to be so good at getting just what she wanted and needed in order to survive. When we were young, she'd get all of our clothes from the Salvation Army and Scott Mission. She knew where to get anything for free in Toronto. She was illiterate, but she knew everyone's phone number. She'd phone information and ask the operator for a number. If the number wasn't listed, she'd say, "You dumb girl!" and hang up. She knew where to get all kinds of things, and this became a big game for her.

But after the stroke, she never wanted to talk about anything other than China. She used to talk about when she was a little girl — how she used to have to go out and look after the cow all day. She was very mischievous, always getting in trouble. She'd always let the cow escape or go to the store and charge candy — that's how she lost all her teeth. Because she was so bad, her mother used to tie her up, hang her from a tree and whip her. I guess they were glad they shipped her off to Canada.

I don't think my mother was bitter about her childhood for she never felt anything about beating us up. She'd hit us with feather dusters, electrical cords and shoes, but it got to the point where she knew she couldn't hurt us. We had this pact that she wasn't going to make us cry. Also, she was only 4' 11", and when we were growing up we were getting too big for her. So she'd have other ways to hurt us since beating was no longer enough. She knew school was very important to us, and she'd threaten to burn our school books. She never carried out her threat though....

My father died when I was twelve. My mother had put him in a home because she couldn't look after him. He was old and incontinent. Because we were so poor, it was a government home — which meant it was pretty awful, a dormitory with a hundred beds. My father had cataracts and he couldn't see. He couldn't speak English. When he died, my mother said he was haunting her. She couldn't stay in the house. So we moved to the Beaches area of Toronto — a middle class neighbourhood, no Chinese at all. No one knew that we were poor. We just pretended to be middle class like everyone else....

IRENE CHU

Irene was born in Shanghai, China, in 1938. She immigrated to Canada in 1963. SHe currently lives in Toronto.

My parents are from very modern families. My mother attended McTeer Girl's School in Shanghai. It was run by American missionaries. My mother's father was a banker who owned three "money houses" in Shanghai. "Money houses" functioned much the same way as trust companies now but were less structured and less regulated.

My paternal grandfather owned thousands of acres of land in Nan Zhong, in Jiangxi province. He was the sole distributor of Mobile Oil for the province. He traded in rice, lumber and salt. Grandfather did quite a bit of business with foreigners.

Jiangxi became the stronghold for the budding Communist Party, and my grandfather's house was taken over by the Kuomintang as headquarters to combat the Communists. The bulk of my father's family migrated to Shanghai.

My father was introduced to my mother through her cousin. They actually dated before marriage. They watched American movies and attended social functions at the French club. I recall in my childhood during the Second World War that most of my father's business associates were Jewish. My father was the first Chinese to obtain a seat in the Shanghai Stock Exchange which was controlled by the British in those days.

Our family was affluent in Shanghai, with servants, a chauffeur, butler and three automobiles. In Hong Kong the family suffered major financial setbacks and emotional turmoil throughout the fifties. My mother became ill with cancer around 1956. She died in 1960 when I was in second year at Hong Kong University.

Hong Kong was never considered as a permanent home to us who fled as "refugees" from the mainland. One by one we left. At present, with the exception of Angela in Seattle, all my immediate family members are in the Toronto area.

JANE WOO

Jane Woo is a pseudonym for a woman born in Victoria, B.C. in 1928. At the time of her interview, she was residing in Winnipeg.

Those days, parents didn't show any kind of affection as they do now. There wasn't the hugging, the loving. It was very rigid, strict and inhibited.... We were very close I suppose, as brothers and sisters at that time. I remember having to hover around one of these big, potbellied stoves to get warm. We'd get up cold and freezing. We'd come down and there's a little pan-type of thing that my mother might have heated up some water in for us to wash ourselves. We'd get dressed by that stove. Sometimes my mother would have porridge cooking on it.

Another memory of my mother is her growing mung beans and bean sprouts to help out when my dad was unemployed. We'd all help with the packaging. It became part of the day. After school we'd help clean the beans before we had dinner....

GRACE LEE

My mother didn't have to do anything except raise the children and be a missus! All the wives of the three nearby households led similar lives. They didn't play *mah jong* or gamble. They liked to wear beautiful clothes and dress up their children. They were very beautiful. My mother didn't even have to do any cooking in those days. All the meals were cooked and sent up by the people in our store. We were really very comfortable.

My father went back to China frequently and all my older brothers were already in Canada. The whole family returned to China when my father retired. I don't know how old he was at that time, but he was quite old. Men in those days all had several wives. My father had three wives. Only my mother didn't have bound feet. My father took a third wife because he consulted a geomancer who said that my mother wouldn't have a long life, so he had better bring in a third wife to look after him.... My mother lived to be ninety-six! You don't know the problems of large families, but my father was very loyal to all his wives and children, treating them all the same. However, I didn't like his authoritarianism. I wanted my freedom.

When I came back to China for a visit after teaching in Canada for a few years, my father was so happy and invited everyone to dinner. I told him that he didn't have to support me because I could earn my own money. So I started to communicate with him. Girls then did not talk to their fathers. I was twenty-nine years old when I went back to see my father after he had chased me away.

Towards the end of his life, my father said I was the best of all of his seventeen children. He finally knew me in the end. I looked after my mother afterwards and she came to live with me in Canada. She was seventy-five and I was forty-five.

MYRTLE WONG

My mother stuck to Chinese tradition — she favoured the boys. This favouritism hurt deeply. Whenever we were involved in some physical fight, even though I was the wounded one, Mother used to ignore me and just rush to the aid of her son and sympathize with him. And I'd be left holding my open wound. Because we were taught filial piety, I didn't express my resentment to my parents ... but I used to cry by myself.

Mother married Dad when she was fourteen. She had her first child at fifteen. She felt lonely in Australia because she couldn't speak English, so I used to take her out and act as her translator. No, we didn't get close. I just did these things for her because it was my duty. I helped her a lot with the housework. She was a fragile type of woman who needed support from someone.

My father was very old-fashioned. He would not let my mother have any say in matters concerning the family. He wanted to make all the decisions — even concerning what to serve dinner guests. He manipulated her like a puppet, giving her no freedom to think for herself.

FERN HUM

Fern was born in Sudbury, Ontario in 1950. At the time of her interview, she was residing in Toronto.

My mother always said that she wanted only one child (laugh). For the first seven years of her marriage, she was pregnant every year! Imagine five little kids who didn't go to school yet! I would have gone nuts! She delivered all of us at home, except for the first one. In those days there wasn't any medicare, so going to the hospital was expensive and my father couldn't afford it.

The Chinese women's group in Sudbury was my mother's

only social outlet. She didn't have much else. The group was formed by a few women in the church who wanted to reach out to the entire Chinese community through the Chinese women, since most of them were at home in those days. No, I don't think they were involved in cultural activities. It was more a social thing. There were probably some Bible lessons involved, I'm not really sure. But it was a the church that most of the Chinese women went to. My mother was the first Chinese woman to come to Sudbury. Shortly after the Exclusion Act was lifted, other Chinese women began coming. But my mother felt quite isolated in the beginning....

My father had a daughter from a common-law marriage which my mother didn't even know about until she came over to Canada. She was very angry when she found out about it. She held bitterness about it until her death a couple of years ago. I think she felt cheated a lot. Many times she said if she had known about certain things before, she would not have married my father.

My parents married here in Canada. According to my mother, my father sent the fare over to China, so she could come to Canada, and she repaid him later on with money she earned from her own bean sprout business — yes, she had a small business by herself. At that time, Chinese food was becoming kind of popular. People were sort of accepting things like chop suey and egg rolls, the kind that you fry with the wonton skin. So she started this little business and managed to make a bit of money.

No, my father didn't see my mother before she came here. There were only pictures exchanged. My mother kept on saying (laugh), "He sent a younger picture." Also, my father was almost fifteen years older than my mother. All these things made my mother very bitter throughout the marriage. I guess my father's illegitimate daughter was topping on the cake. There were many complicated things in their marriage — and in our family life. But I think of my mother as a very brave person who didn't waver under these circumstances. She held her own ... and was very loyal. I mean, nowadays, a lot of people, once they hear this, they'd ask for a divorce. I don't know if she *could* have left. I don't think she had enough money to get a fare back to China. I don't think she would have known who to contact to get a ticket for the ship. There weren't many travel agents who spoke Chinese. And how would she have been able to re-establish herself back in China — or even Hong Kong? No, she was more or less stuck in Canada.

She came into a very small mining community in which the majority of the people were English speaking. There were very few facilities where she could speak Chinese and get her points across. She had to stay where she was and deal with the situation and try to learn some English and maybe make some headway that way.

Later as a teenager and into adulthood, I would hear more of the frustration she faced. She didn't say too much when I was younger, except that I knew she didn't like my half-sister. She wouldn't allow her to live with us, so my half-sister went from foster home to foster home — and, consequently, did not have a very stable family life. Occasionally, between foster homes, my father would bring my sister to our home, hoping that my mother would eventually accept his other daughter. But I don't think she ever did.

At first I was angry with my father for putting my mother in this situation. I also felt angry with my mother for rejecting her step-daughter. I thought that my mother should have been a bit more forgiving and allow my older sister to be part of our family even though she was not of the same mother.

When I got older, when I understood a bit more Chinese history, I was able to have some sympathy for my father. I know a couple of other Chinese families in Sudbury who have il-legitimate children from the fathers' common-law relationships with white women, particularly French-Canadian women. Since most of these men didn't have *Chinese* spouses here in Canada, some of them took up common-law marriages because there was a need for some kind of loving relationship.

JEAN LEE

My mother was old-fashioned. She thought that when we marry, we're no longer Hongs — so she gave everything to my brother. When my dad died he didn't have a will. At that time I signed over some papers to my mother, so she could have the building and collect the rent for her lifetime. And she promised to give it back to us — because before Dad died, he said, "Boys are the same as girls. You must treat them the same because if it wasn't for the girls in this family, we would be broke and on welfare." We, the girls, were the ones who paid off the mortgage on the building! But my mother told us she changed her will: "Now I'm going to leave two thirds to Sui because he's a Hong, to carry on the family name." So we figured one third between me and my sister, okay ... but when she died a few years ago, we found out it was one third split between me and my sister *and* my brother's wife and three children! Ha! So that really left him with ninety percent and us with just five percent! My sister and I were very upset.

I guess my mother felt she had to look after her son. He was the only son left, since two other sons were killed in Europe during the war. Then the youngest one was killed in a motorcycle accident. So she sort of doted on her remaining son. His was an arranged marriage because he'd married a woman with a poor reputation and got divorced. Mother paid for his divorce and sent him to China and arranged for him to marry this second wife.... My sister and I are considering taking the case to court and having the will broken. That was ... *really* a raw deal!

VICTORIA YIP

Victoria was born in Victoria, B.C. in 1911. At the time of her interview, she was residing in Vancouver.

Most of the old-fashioned Chinese, they like boys better than girls, but my uncle and my father valued the girls far more than the boys. I know our family was unusual. I mean, for instance, every Sunday we used to hire a taxi to go to Beacon Hill Park or Mount Douglas Park to look at the view. None of the other Chinese families did that. My father knew all the plants and he'd show us. We went to the hills to pick green onions, wild green onions. Victoria is the only place I know that has them, and they're really delicious. We'd bring them home and made Chinese pancakes. You grated potato and put in pork and dried shrimp chopped up and the green onions. We would invite all our friends up, so we would be making it the whole day. I think my father did extra because my mother had died so young — when I was only eleven. My father was a very unusual man. We always went every Sunday to the cemetery which is near the sea. Then we would gather the shells, clams and seaweed and bring them all home.

EDUCATION WAS THE MOST IMPORTANT THING

VICTORIA YIP

I was born in Chinatown, but we moved close to Victoria High School when I was very young because my father said he wanted us to be near a high school, an elementary school and a primary school. I lost my mother at the age of eleven and we lived with a very good aunt and uncle and their children. My uncle was like my father, very interested in education. They both considered it the most important thing for their children. They studied all their lives. And my mother had been a school teacher in China, so she stressed the importance of education to us too when we were younger.

Most of the old-fashioned Chinese prefer boys to girls, but my uncle and my father valued the girls far more than the boys. They felt that it was best for us girls to be as self-sufficient as possible. Don't forget, when you grow up, there's no white people going to hire you.

I liked high school, but I found studying very hard. I liked it because, like my father and uncle, I believed that education was the most important thing. I wanted to learn as much as I could.

I also enjoyed my Chinese school which I did not start until the age of fourteen. I was surprised that I liked it. I really worked hard and I had very dedicated teachers. I loved to read too. When I'd cook supper, I'd put the book open above the stove. And when I was going to Chinese school and we had to walk over a mile from our place to Chinatown, I always had a book to read as I walked — because that was the only available time I had. My favourite subject was writing essays and stories — I guess because I'm a dreamer.

Another thing I remember about Chinese school was what we called the Self Disciplining Club — or *gee gee wu*. The teacher didn't have to discipline us. We disciplined ourselves. If the teacher caught you talking in class, he would write down the time and date you were talking. Then every Saturday afternoon we had a meeting from one to three, and we'd say, "Okay, you talked, then are you guilty or not guilty?" We had a judge. If you were guilty you were fined one cent.

Then at night time on Saturday from six to nine, we had a debating society and speech making. You could either make a speech or do story-telling. I was very, very shy when I was young. I think that these extra-curricular activities forced me to stand up and open my mouth to talk. That gave me a lot of confidence in myself.

GRACE LEE

A friend of mine had advised me to go to the missionary school which conferred degrees. I wanted to work and it would be difficult for me without a degree, so I insisted on going to the missionary school. I wanted to go out to work because the more the Chinese families think that girls could not study and achieve anything aside from getting married, the more I wanted to show them that it could be done. I wanted to win. Ai-ya! It was very sad, really. I laugh at it now, but at the time it was very, very sad. I was extremely brave.

After I finished my schooling in China, I knew I wanted to go abroad because I had been chased out of my home by my father after I became a Christian. It was a very hard time. I didn't have any money. I had to borrow money for my tuition to complete high school and my teachers' program. My father wouldn't lend me the money. He wanted me to get married when I was around eighteen, before I went to the missionary school. But I've never married. In his mind, I was ruining his reputation by seeking freedom and refusing to get married.

My thinking was not influenced by what I learned at school. It's just that I couldn't stand the archaic thinking of the Chinese that females shouldn't study — that they would never succeed. So I was very angry at that time. Why could all the boys in our family go to school and the girls couldn't? I wanted to break away from that.

I had always wanted to learn. I still do. I value my freedom very much. When I was a teacher I would try to steal some time in between my teaching to take lessons myself. I studied English because I didn't know how to speak the language, even though I had taken English in China. I knew how to read, but I couldn't speak it. I paid two dollars an hour for my lessons. Now I can understand and speak English. I'm not afraid to meet anyone!

Later when I was older, after I took my students home at twelve, I would rush through my lunch and go to my typing class. I had to teach again at four p.m. I made time the same way for my piano lessons. I was in my fifties then. I took typing because the doctor said I would be blind in about six months, and I was determined to learn everything I could. I used to read medical books at night too, so I could correctly use medical terms when translating for Chinese patients. I'm very happy now because I have a lot of things to amuse myself with — thanks to my learning about things when I was young.

I went back to China to see everyone one last time before the blindness set in. And when I returned to Canada, I took up music, learning to play the violin, the accordion, the harmonica and the flute.

ANNE FONG

Anne Fong is a pseudonym for a woman who was born in Alberta in 1933. At the time of the interview, she was residing in Calgary.

Oh, the school life! Then we got some respect! (laugh) All the Chinese children excelled in school. I guess that's one thing that the *lo fan* respected. My mother would tell this story often. The *lo fan* would ask how come my parents could hardly read or write or speak English, yet their children could understand everything and excel at school? They said that the banker's son had to have a private tutor, and he still couldn't pass. So they always marvelled at that.

At school the other kids would want help from my brothers and sisters. They'd ask them to tutor. I remember one sister saying that the other kids wanted to copy her work. They'd say things like, "Sit still so I can see your answers." When I went to school they had grades four, five and six in one room. There would be thirty to thirty-five students altogether.

The Chinese had hopes that their children would have a better life. Their respect for education helped their children overcome discrimination. They respect the printed word. My father had only a few years of school. My mother was illiterate. But as a child growing up, we always had books. Now where they came from, I don't know. I remember many, many happy hours as a child reading Dickens, Bronte and all those English authors.

In those days, there were very few Chinese at university. I felt that I didn't want to be a secretary. I didn't want to be a nurse. My mother still had the old perspective. A girl should have something to do until she gets married. She suggested hairdressing and secretarial work. Her suggestions probably made me more determined than ever to get a degree and have a career because I felt that a woman could do anything that a man could do. So I went back to university for five years and became a social worker.

VELMA CHAN

My sister and I started school together. Our house was over a mile from the school. We had to walk every morning, and even when the winter was severe. My mother, not being conversant in Canadian ways, used to send us off with our lunch buckets, our little lard pails of lunch. We'd eat our lunch at recess and then come home, not knowing any better — no one ever told us we were to stay the day. I thought it was rather silly: bring your lunch, eat it at school and then walk home. We carried on until finally I got wise to it. Mother didn't know and nobody told her that the children were to stay there all day.

During the Depression, I took a year out from high school to help my father because he was having a rough time. I sold vegetables, and together we raised a little more money for household expenses. Then he paid me the money to go the last year of high school. My father worked very hard. I wanted to help him. He was thinking of a rosier future for the children, so I didn't begrudge the hardship at all.

I was the only Chinese girl at the high school in Merritt. And my father paid four dollars a month for my education. After graduation, a lot of the girls went into either nursing or teaching because those were considered proper professions. But I was told not to go by so-called "leading citizens" of Merritt. They told my father that it was no use letting me go on to higher education since I'd *never* get a job. Hmph, believe it or not! My parents thought it was just as wise not to spend the extra money sending me out-of-town to school. I was envious of the girls who either went into nursing or teaching. That was quite something to achieve, but I didn't go.

LIL LEE

Schooling wasn't that big a thing during the Depression. The most important thing was to go out to work and help support the family. We weren't really encouraged that much to go for higher education. We did manage to go to high school, but we didn't have the resources to put any of us through university.

High school was okay, but quite a few of my Chinese friends dropped out. By the time I graduated, there was just one other Chinese person — a boy who graduated with me. I guess my family wasn't quite as old-fashioned as some of those other Chinese families. My paternal grandfather was quite an independent businessman. My mother's father was a bookkeeper, and he always stressed the importance of education, although my mother didn't have a chance to be educated. It was discouraged because she was a girl. However, my mother's brother was encouraged to go to school. I suppose that some of the girls who didn't finish school had reached a certain age to be married off. Their families probably thought that, instead of wasting their time going to school, perhaps it would be better for these girls to get married to someone who could support them.

SANDRA LEE

Sandra was born in Victoria, B.C. in 1937. At the time of her interview, she was residing in Victoria, B.C.

My parents had to pay for Chinese school — three or five dollars a month. We didn't really learn much, I'm sad to say. I wish I had learned more. I enjoyed Chinese school because everybody wanted to play when there were all these Chinese kids together. I still keep in touch with friends I made from Chinese school. While we were there we had opportunities to do other things, like the drill team — the Victoria Chinese Girls' Drill Team.[1] We were in groups of sixteen and we did marching formations in Chinese costumes imported from Hong Kong. It lasted for about three or four years in the early 1950s. It was fun performing in parades and at different public functions.

ROSE LUMB

Rose was born in Victoria, B.C. in 1928. At the time of her interview, she was residing in Victoria, B.C.

School life was very enjoyable to me. I only wished that our parents could have afforded to buy encyclopedias and better study books for us. But our family was quite poor. We also had to go to Chinese school after our regular English school, and it was very hard to get to the library to do our studying because the libraries closed quite early in those days.

The Chinese school was there for us so that we wouldn't forget our Chinese background, our parents' culture. It wasn't what I'd call serious study, but I'm very pleased that I went because, even to this day, I still attend a Chinese church and I can speak Cantonese fairly well — even though I can't read all the Chinese words.

EDUCATION WAS THE MOST IMPORTANT THING

CAROLINE CHAN

Caroline was born in Truro, New Brunswick in 1959. At the time of her interview, she was residing in St. John, New Brunswick.

When I was young, my schoolmates were rotten, really rotten. When I was in grade one, one girl didn't like Chinese people at all, so she pushed me — she pushed me off the stairs at school. I rolled down the stairs on my face. The whole right side of my face was all scratched up. My mother was *really* mad. But it was just one of those things, you know.

Our school was a real melting pot. Some of St. John's wealthiest went to school there — and some of St. John's poorest. Where we lived was in a really nice part of town. But just below our home was a low-income apartment development. My mother always told me not to go down there because the people were swearing, drinking, taking drugs and beating each other. But it wasn't just those people who weren't nice. Even some of the wealthier kids were not nice.

I guess things got better around junior high. The kids may still feel the same way, but they won't be as vocal about it. All of a sudden they realized you had feelings. In grade seven, this one girl *never* liked me — never, never, never. And in gym I was very shy — my mother always taught me to be very modest. So I'd go to the washroom cubicles and change. Then some of the other girls in my class would make fun of me. And this particular girl, the one who *couldn't stand* me, actually went up to the girl who called me a "chink" and hit her. Then she said, "Don't say those things. It's not nice. You'll hurt her feelings. She's a human being. Leave her alone." It really shocked me, but she was still never nice to me. She just didn't like me — but she never allowed anyone to abuse me.

MAY CHOW

I was actually too old for public school when I arrived here at the age of sixteen, but it happened that there was a Chinese teacher in primary school. I sat in her grade one class for a few months, learning ABCs. Then I went on to grade four. A few months later I went to grade five — and a half a year later I was in grade eight. I was happy but very bored and I missed my mother who had not yet arrived from Hong Kong. I studied very hard, trying to catch up in English. All the other courses were easy because I had already learned it all in China.

I was the only Chinese at the school. The students were nice to me. Some girls would tutor English to me after school. The teachers were very nice to me too. I still keep in touch with them. I stopped going to school after grade nine because I had to help support the family.

LINDA LEE

The problem of higher education for girls became a question with high school. All three of us were good students. May wanted to go to college, but our family didn't have the money to send the girls. Some of the older members of the Chinese community thought it would be a waste of money to send girls because it was expected that we would be getting married soon. I remember listening to people tell my father about the futility of sending us to college. This would be about '65 or '66. My father was very much aware of the fact that we were living in a different time and country. He decided that if we could find a way to pay for college ourselves, we could go. He said he'd be able to help us a bit. But basically, if we wanted to go and could pay our own way, that was just fine with him.

We knew that our father was under quite a bit of pressure. But at that time, we were not the first girls to ask. Mary Mohammed was ahead of us. There was a big uproar when she wanted to go. So by our time, someone else had at least gotten people used to the idea that the girls might want to go.

When I went to university I majored in English. All three of us were on scholarships and each of us worked during the summer. The Chinese community had nothing to say about that. Because the Chinese have a great respect for learning, I sensed that they were proud of us in the end.

JEAN LEE

For us, school was good because we had no problems there. We made friends. We stood at the top of our class. My sisters and I were considered quite clever in school. I think that was because we had nothing else to distract our attention. While the Canadian kids played outside and stuff like that, we stayed home — either working or doing school work.

FERN HUM

My parents sort of felt we had to go to Chinese school after English school. I went for about three or four years when I was probably between eight and eleven. It was basically a group of men in the community who started the school. Actually, they had a teacher from Hong Kong come and she spoke Cantonese — whereas all the Chinese in Sudbury spoke Toisanese or Sung wei. I spoke Sung wei. I would come home to my mother and read all my lessons to her. There's a difference in pronunciation, and my mother would say, "Oh dear, you're learning the pronunciation all wrong there." (laugh) But we were made to go to Chinese school. I don't know how much my parents paid for it, but we had to go five days a week, from five to seven.

We didn't learn very much Chinese at Chinese school (laugh). I remember we had to use this black ink to write letters. My brother would take it and put marks on his face and make moustaches. All the grades were in one room. There were only about two or three people in each grade. So all these kids would be playing in one room (laugh). I probably learned a few numbers and how to write my name — but that's about it.

IRENE CHU

There are five of us girls and one boy, the youngest in our family, who was born severely retarded. My parents placed the emphasis on higher education. They never pressured their daughters about dating or marriage — they simply encouraged us to do well academically.

My eldest sister Isabelle majored in Psychology. Yvonne, the third sister, is a systems analyst. Stella, the fourth, did a Masters in Mathematics and went on to study Actuarial Science. My youngest sister, Angela, has a Phd. in Sociology. I majored in English Literature and completed one and a half years of a M.A. at McGill University. But because of babysitting problems I didn't complete my thesis. It's been over twenty years — maybe I'll resume the work as my retirement project....

DR. LINDA LEE

No one in Cabbagetown went to university. You just learned to be a secretary or mechanic or something. But school was important to me because I got approval from the teachers. The teachers would say, "Oh, that's very good," whereas my mother thought that if you didn't get straight As, you were stupid. She didn't understand anything about what was going on. My older sisters used to sign the report cards and absence notes. My mother didn't know anything unless we didn't do well. I skipped a grade in grade eight and caught up with my sister who was a year older.

I'd always wanted to be a secretary (laugh), so I said I wanted to go to Monarch Park and learn how to type and be a good secretary, instead of going to Malvern, the school closest to us. Malvern was a collegiate, so you don't go there unless you plan to go to university. But at the last minute, my sister said to me, "You're too smart to go to Monarch Park — come to Malvern with me." We had won all these academic awards in grade eight. We used to get a lot of praise from our teachers. I think that's why we worked hard. My sister and I are the only two in the family to finish grade thirteen.

I went to Scarborough College, University of Toronto. That was a hassle because we were on welfare. Since I was only seventeen, they were supposed to cover me. But a social worker came to say that they would still cover me only if I were going to a technical school or community college. They cut me off because I wanted to go to a university. Then my mother didn't want me to go. "You can already read and write — what more is there? You go out and make some money. Why do you want to go to school?"

I attended university on student loans and the money I earned from my part-time work. I used to have to pay my mother room and board too.

When I came home from school, my brothers who were still living at home would say, "Well, college kid, what did you learn today?" I thought, if I just got a B.A. or B.Sc., they'd say "So what, you still can't do anything." So I started thinking about applying to some professional school. Everybody at Scarborough College was applying to dentistry and medicine. I missed the medicine aptitude test, so I took the dentistry one.

Dental school at the University of Toronto was terrible (laugh). Awful. I wouldn't do it again. There were 125 in the class and there were only eight girls. There was one other Chinese girl, though. It was just torture. You started at eight and finished at six every day — and then you had to do your homework. A lot of it was stressful because it was physical work. I used to think, oh, I'll wait until they throw me out because I can't quit — my family would kill me if I quit. Actually, I won some awards and was really surprised.

Note

1. Chinese Girls' Drill Team — Established by the Victoria Chinese Public School in the 1940s, it performed in various parades and holiday events during the 1940s and 1950s.

WORK, WORK, WORK!

VELMA CHAN

As far back as I can remember, it has always been a steady routine of work, work, work. First thing in the morning, my mother would get us up at about seven. We'd have our breakfast and my father would take us to town in a horse-drawn wagon to collect food left over from restaurants and butcher shops to feed our pigs on the farm (laugh). My mother used to cook up what they call the "slop" to feed the hogs. The rest of the day my mother would work in the house or on the farm with a child in her arms or on her back.

MARY WONG

Mary was born in Hamilton, Ontario, in 1919. She continues to reside in Hamilton.

When I was in high school it was very difficult for Chinese girls to find jobs. We'd go pick strawberries in the summertime — make a couple of dollars. But I mean, there weren't any jobs around for us — not until during the war. Before World War Two, you wouldn't see Chinese people working in factories. Not in Hamilton. So I was lucky to get a job at my sister's restaurant in Fort Erie.

I started my own restaurant after I was married. My mother used to say, you know, *hoo sang* were not so ambitious, not like people born in China. They figured that we didn't have any backbone. I mean a few of the older Chinese people said that I wouldn't last six months — and I'm still here (laugh) — forty years later! I guess I succeeded in showing people that I could stick to something. Coming from a large family, we all worked very hard — and we all helped each other. I mean, I have worked very, very hard — harder than the rest of my family.

I'd get up at about five in the morning ... and I'd work until we closed — with only two hours sleep. Every morning I'd make about fifty lunches. Like, I had to cut the bread, cut the bacon, make the coffee. Then it was lunch hour and we'd be really busy. Then maybe around two, I'd go and lie down for a couple of hours before preparing for the supper hour. It seemed like I didn't do anything else but work.

Since we opened the restaurant in 1943, I've been the one in control of the business. It has been at least twenty years of just work, work, work. We've only closed the restaurant for a holiday once — for a week.

When I wasn't working in the restaurant, I was doing community work. Through the years, if someone in the Chinese community needed to go to the doctor or lawyer — or whatever, I'd go as a translator. Then I'd have to get some extra help in the restaurant. The odd time I'd also go to court to do some interpreting, and the court would pay me a couple of dollars ... which helped.

One time I got so involved with my community activities that I almost lost the restaurant. If you're in business, you have to take care of your business. So I smartened up and made sure that my business was always running smoothly.

VICTORIA YIP

After high school, I worked in two jobs. The doors to better jobs were closed to Chinese people at that time. No white people were going to hire Chinese, so I went to work in a Chinese grocery store, from eight to five. Then from five to eight in the evening, I'd go to the Chinese school and teach youngsters. I loved teaching, and it just happened that the Freemasons[1] had a school and my father was the principal, so naturally ... (laugh)

I kept both jobs until I married at the age of twenty. I hated the fruit store job, but I loved the teaching job. And I loved those six year-old kids. Sometimes they gave me heartaches, but most of the time it was a joy.

When I came to Vancouver (after living on Tuxeda Island for twenty-six years), I started working full-time in a housewares store in Chinatown. I was in my late fifties. Lots of people said, "Oh, you must be nervous about going to work after staying at home all these years with your three kids." But I wasn't nervous. I couldn't see any difficulties — just go head on — learn, that's all! I'd already been working in the community anyway. That's why I say volunteer work is really very, very good for women. It gives you self-confidence. And that's the most important thing to have.

I've always believed that if the men can do it, the women can do it. Actually, there's nothing to keep the women from doing what they want in this world. About 120 years ago, my aunt went to Peking to go to school. She brought us up with modern ideas. She was a terrific woman. She'd let us watch movies and Chinese opera. We'd go swimming and dancing. She let us cut our hair. So we were raised in a liberated atmosphere!

MAE LEE

It was the early 1950s when I started working for Avon, selling door-to-door. I had a gall bladder operation and I couldn't do the heavy work I used to do at the greenhouse. My last baby was six years old when I started with Avon. The kids came home from school at three-thirty. I'd be back home by four.

In 1955 I began working for Investors Syndicate of Canada. I found out about it through the husband of one of my Avon customers. I was making over $400 a month with Avon, so I was a bit leery about joining Investors — since I didn't know anything about selling stocks. I was with them for ten years, until 1964. I earned really good money with Investors. If I hadn't joined them, I wouldn't be where I am today. I was the first woman with the company across Canada, and I learned a lot from those men — four-thirty every Monday afternoon I'd sit with them in a meeting. Today I know just as much as they do about investing money.... Now all my children automatically save money.

SANDRA LEE

Sandra is the daughter of Mae Lee.

When we were younger, we worked in a greenhouse for a dollar a day. Then from grade five to grade twelve, we worked in a grocery store. All the money we earned went into Mom's pocket. You know, these days the kids get to keep their money, but Mom was strict with us. She forced us to save.

I don't regret that I had to work so hard when I was growing up. It built a basic groundwork for me. The experience of working all the time shows you what you're capable of doing. If you ever had to do it again, you could, if you pushed yourself to do it.

After the crisis of my divorce, I came back fighting. I went through all my emotional and financial stress on my own. I went out to work. I was a domestic. You name it, I did it. This was just a couple of years ago. No, I don't have any kids. I've realized from looking around me that life is too short to keep working double shifts. I now work only six hours a day in a grocery store. Wages aren't high, but I'm happy. That's the most important thing. I've also realized that you can live on very little if you have to. It's using your resources....

Mother would have liked to sort of say, you do this, you do that, about our careers, but after a while, she realized that each of us has to find our own little niche. Most mothers aspire to have their children be doctors, lawyers, accountants — that's typical. But I think if you can't go that way — if one wants to be a ditch digger instead.... As long as one is happy, that's more important.

MAY CHEUNG

When I first came to Toronto in 1956, I didn't go out to work. Hardly any jobs were available for women then. Few women worked outside the home. I stayed home until my youngest son was ten. My husband worked in his uncle's laundry. Then we opened our own laundry in 1979. I helped in the laundry.

Now I work as a sewing machine operator. When my children grew older, I didn't want them to play around outside all the time, so I took another job and asked them to help in the laundry after school.

It was very hard to get this job. I went to many different factories, but they wouldn't hire me. One day, I saw an ad in front of the factory across from our laundry. I rushed across the street. Oh, I was so surprised when I got it. The hourly wages were only

$1.50 — really! That was 1973.... After working for so many years, I still only get $5.30 per hour. But I get paid by piece work, seldom by hourly wages.

We've been unionized for about three years. It was difficult for the union to rally the support of the workers. Many did not want to join. But the government said there were so many workers in our factory that we had to join. So we finally sent a few representatives and formed the union. Well, I think unions are generally good — for people who don't have good jobs. But for more capable workers like me, I don't think the union is so good.

Before, I used to be able to talk to the boss whenever I felt there was something wrong, right? But now, having worked for over ten years, I still get the same wages as a newcomer — I'm not happy about that. The union says it has to protect the newcomers. About four years ago we got an increase of fifty cents per hour after we joined the union. This brought our wages up to five dollars per hour. Any new employee would also get five dollars per hour. It's not fair. I think piece work rates are also unfair. When there was no union, I could talk directly to the boss.... The wages are better at the factory where my sister works. But I haven't tried to get a job there since my factory is closer to home — and despite everything, I still earn quite a bit by piece work. But when I think about it, it really gets to me sometimes.

Every day, I work from seven-thirty in the morning until five in the evening — nine hours a day! Then I help out a bit in the family laundry, depending on the amount of work. Then I go home and prepare dinner.

But of course, it is good for women to go out and work. I was fed up with being stuck at home for so many years. Working outside the home, you meet people. I have always wanted to go out to work, but before I couldn't do it because I was tied down with the children.

CAROLINE CHAN

When I graduated from university in 1981, I really didn't know what I was going to do. So my father offered me a chance to come and see how his restaurant operated. It consumed all my time. I mean I worked *all the time*. There was a lot to learn about accounts, books, bank statements. I had to learn a lot about handling people. I'm sure that the girls who worked at the restaurant would vouch for the fact that I learned to be a little more careful with people. I learned a lot about myself. I had to manage to learn how to talk to businessmen — not to be shy. Now I'm not shy at all.

You have to be sure of yourself when you talk to businessmen. When you say something you have to mean it. You need to learn to be firm, without being nasty or bitchy. I'm still working on that (laugh). It's like anyone who is the shy wallflower suddenly being thrust into the middle of the dance floor. Well, she's got to learn how to dance — or else she's going to look stupid. So I guess I decided to learn how to dance (laugh).

LIL LEE

In those days it was difficult to find a job because a lot of places weren't hiring Chinese. Even if you had the training to be a secretary, and you applied for a job in a bank or office, it was very hard, especially in a small town like Nanaimo. It was funny how you sort of just accepted it — not being hired because you're Chinese. It was almost futile to really fight for a job when you knew you would never get it anyway. So you either opened your own business or went for higher education. But in those days, very few women went to university. There weren't any Chinese doctors, lawyers and insurance companies — not like today. That's why a lot of Chinese families had their own businesses — restaurants, groceries, laundries, or something like that — create your own employment, in other words.

I worked in the family business. It took up a lot of my time when I was young. Then when I was in my mid-twenties, I decided that I should have a life of my own. So I moved to Vancouver in 1954.

When I arrived in Vancouver, I went to work at the Bank of Nova Scotia. The assistant manager was Chinese, probably the first Chinese in such as position. The manager was a Canadian. Over fifty percent of the business was Chinese, so they needed Chinese workers. Three out of the four tellers would be Chinese since most of the customers didn't know how to speak English. Then later I found it quite repetitious and boring. I quit after a year there, when I got married.

When I had my third child we got rid of our family grocery store. Then three years later I felt that I'd stayed home long enough and I went out to work in a law office for a number of years. Later I helped my husband with his store, Chinese Arts and Crafts.

SHIRLEY WELSH

When I was twelve or thirteen, we moved to Bengough, Saskatchewan, only about thirty miles from the Montana border — and I started working in the family restaurant. A day's routine was very tiring. For about an hour before the bus came to get me in the morning for school, I had to wait on tables. Then I came home for lunch — and I had to wait on tables again. Then after school from four-thirty until we closed around midnight, I would have to work. On Fridays and Saturdays we closed at two in the morning. Then we had to open up again at eight in the morning.... You try to do your homework, it's next to impossible because there're always interruptions.

I didn't resent the fact that I was the only one in the family helping my parents. But I guess there was resentment when I felt that I worked so hard without any pay. After closing, Dad usually gave us, maybe, $20 or $30 to spend. But I didn't see it as paying me for the work. I guess I expected to get a cheque on paydays like I saw other people get, but he gave me cash instead, you know. I even went on strike about three or four times! I refused to work. I refused to eat. Well, we talked. Dad tried to reason with me, saying, "Shirley, $20 is a lot of money. Other kids don't get that much — they only get about $5 or $10 for helping around the family farm." He was quite reasonable, but at that time I didn't see it like that. I remember one time I made a sign and picketed in the restaurant (laugh) — "Teenage Free Labour" (laugh). It was ridiculous, the talk of the town, you know.

Now that I'm older, I realize how selfish and foolish I was. But at that time ... my feelings were hurt and I felt so insulted —

147

because I wasn't getting paid. It's just that I felt I had put so many long hours into it, plus going to school. I couldn't participate in sports like my sisters when I was growing up because I was constantly working.

Finally, my father said, "Okay, I'll pay you — I'll pay you $200." And I thought, "Oh, that's a lot of money!" But my dad said, "Now you have to pay room and board." I agreed, as long as he agreed to pay me $200 every month. Then he said, "I'll pay you, but now when you have your pop and chips, or chocolate bars after school, *you* have to pay for that now." I was in a deficit before the month was up! (laugh) — he just wanted to get all his money back.

MAY MAH

After I gave birth to my first baby, I didn't just stay at home. Since our life was not that good, I took up some work when there was a chance. My husband ran a greenhouse owned by his father, so I helped him out there. It was a partnership business, so they employed a lot of workers — like women my age who couldn't find jobs elsewhere. My wages were very low — fifty cents per hour when I first started. No, I did not mind about the wages. It was a sort of family business. Wages in general were very low then for women — like women who washed dishes only earned $60 a month, working ten hours a day, six days a week. During busy times, I sometimes had to work a dozen hours a day — sixteen to seventeen hours a day was normal! We had to work even longer hours in spring — more customers came for bedding plants.

When the partners started to argue, I looked for another job. I got a job in a restaurant — a Chinese "chop suey" restaurant. My friend introduced me to that job. Working there was so-so. I worked as a cashier and receptionist eight hours a day — walking back and forth for eight hours with high heels on, pretty tiring. My wages at the restaurant were not very high, but the boss treated me well — even called me his "adopted daughter" from time to time. I earned $130 a month. That was 1963. Then $10 was deducted each month for meals. I worked there for only ten months. I resigned when I went back to Hong Kong to see my mother.

MARY MOHAMMED

Mary was born in Halifax, Nova Scotia in 1931. At the time of her interview, she was still residing in Halifax.

I remember one time I applied for a summer job in a store. The manager, this Canadian guy, tried to make a pass at me (laugh). You know, he'd take me into the backroom to show me something — and then he tried to get fresh. I mean, gee, that's not a place to be working in. I headed towards the front, where it was safer. But the funny thing is that he had the nerve to say I wouldn't fit in because I was Chinese, you know? Wasn't that awful? He hires you, tries to get fresh with you, and then he says, no, it won't work out because I'm Chinese — the public wouldn't accept me (laugh). I was sixteen. That experience left a bitter taste in my mouth. I was afraid to go on another job interview. You don't know what could happen. I was lucky I came out all right.

JEAN LEE

I remember I was working even before I started school. I used to go down to the restaurant when I was very young and stand on a box to do the dishes. Later I waited on tables. I remember when we went to high school, I used to work until two in the morning, sometimes three, go to bed and then get up at eight for school.

We had it rough, but it didn't do us any harm. I wasn't angry with my parents. We understood the situation, and we knew what had to be done. It's just a sense of responsibility. You had to help out when things were tough. We grew up during the Depression days. Almost everyone was on welfare.

The unemployed people would go to city hall and get a ticket worth 11¢ for breakfast, and 16¢ for dinner. They were allowed two meals a day. They'd pay us with these tickets and we'd give them eggs, toast and coffee. For dinner they'd get a bowl of soup, beef stew, bread, butter and coffee. The next day we'd take all the

149

tickets to city hall and cash them in for money to buy food for the following day.

I continued to work in the restaurant after I was married. But then when the business was sold, I got a job as a secretary/book-keeper for a Chinese person. Then I worked for a dry cleaning company as a bookkeeper and later for a lawyer. Then I got a job working in a bank. My employer told me I was the smartest person they had ever had there. He said Chinese girls made the best workers.

When Eddy came back from overseas service, we started our own marine store. We sell boats, motors, boating accessories. Business has been very good and we are highly respected. We opened in 1958 and we've been there ever since. We have about eight employees, but I'm still at the store from eleven to four.

SHIN MEI LIN

Campbellton was a friendly, small town with only 9,000 people. I was the first to open a Chinese store. Before that I worked in the hospital as a nurse. I started at three a.m. and finished at eleven. Then I would pick up my baby from the sitter. The two older ones were at school.

Finding a job was very easy. But because I couldn't speak English well, I didn't want to be in charge of registration at the hospital. I was happy to take another position for less pay. So I worked the night shift. I came home to watch soap operas and learn English. I changed to the afternoon shift when my baby grew older — because at night the patients were all asleep, so I couldn't practise my English.

GRACE LEE

I was warned that students here would be very difficult to dis-cipline. They said a small woman such as me should watch out. But on my first day at the Chinese Canadian Benevolent Associa-tion,[2] I was very surprised at how obedient and diligent the students were. Most of them were boys — some seventeen or eighteen years old.

I was liked by the principal and the teachers. The school had three other teachers, but I was the only woman. I taught there for three years until I returned to China again for a year. I wanted to prove to my father that a girl could make her own living.

A lot of places in Canada offered me contracts, but I told myself I'd accept the first offer I received. I've always trusted God with my fate. The offer from the Presbyterian Church was the first one, so I agreed to work for them, teaching kindergarten and primary school.

I was not only expected to teach them — I also had to take these children back home at noon when school finished. Nobody would believe we had so many responsibilities. I was paid $70 a month. I had to be very frugal. I rented a room for $15 a month. And I didn't know how to cook, so I had my meals outside. A decent meal in those days was about forty-five cents.

I also had to go visit the families of my students every Friday. Women in those days didn't go out to work, so I would visit their homes to talk to them about their children. Many of these parents were illiterate, so we started English classes for them. The initial response was from older immigrants. Later we had English classes for the younger women from China who spoke no English at all. I did everything there. The more I worked, the happier I got. I had to make doctor's appointments for them, take them to their lawyer's offices, and so on.... When you saw all these people who needed help, you'd help them. I am like this. I told them that they didn't have to pay me anything — only if they wanted to.

I worked at the Presbyterian Church for thirty-four years. I've been retired now for over twenty years. Towards the end, I couldn't see. But the children would help me up the stairs, lay out my books, hand me the chalk and pull the blinds down to keep out the glare.

My students are all grown up now, but they still remember what it was like when I taught them in kindergarten. The mothers used to tell me that their children wouldn't listen to them, but they listened to me. My work was very gratifying to me. I knew I was helping people. I taught three generations of students. Because of these precious experiences, I forgot about returning to China.

ROSE LUMB

When I was about six or seven, some of my brothers and sisters moved to Vancouver to look for work, so the younger ones of us had our share of duties. When I was twelve, I actually had to work in a neighbour's grocery store from eight-thirty in the morning until midnight — for very little. And we all had to pitch in and help with the household chores. I remember scrubbing the clothes in the bathtub with a washboard. We also had to go pick berries and work on farms. I remember going to farms with my mother as early as eight years old, helping in whatever way I could. This was during summer holidays, of course. We were just taken along, rather than left with babysitters. In those days, parents always took their children everywhere.... We had a very tough time during the Depression. So many mouths to feed. But we just managed somehow without *ever* having to ask for welfare or help from anybody....

When I graduated from high school, the school counsellor asked me what kind of work I would like to do. I said to her, "Well you know, the Chinese Canadians have a *very* tough time getting jobs. We work so hard at school, but when we get out, the opportunity is not there for us." So something seemed to have happened there because I was then sent to three different job interviews. I was finally chosen to work at the Canadian Imperial Bank of Commerce. I enjoyed the job because I was able to help a lot of the Chinese men who used to come in. I was also able to draw many Chinese customers from other banks. They used to ask me to help them send drafts back to Hong Kong or China. Sometimes after banking hours, I'd help some of them with their English. Because a lot of them did not have children here, they didn't know where else to turn for help.

There were many times when I felt discrimination because I was a woman. One instance of that at the bank was when the junior boys who started there got more pay than the women.... There were always opportunities I could have pursued, but then the Chinese men would say, "Oh well. The women should be at home more." Instead of giving us the confidence we needed to do the things we wanted to do, they seemed to give us discouragement. Oh, just some of the men in the community — they sort of felt that we women were there only to serve the tea and cater to them.

I chose to stay home to raise my children for eleven years, but I helped my husband do bookkeeping at home. After the eleven years, I helped him run the motel business we owned at that time. When my husband got involved in municipal politics, I had to run the motel myself. Motel work was very hard. You had to clean all the units out and greet the customers. It was from early morning until late at night. The customers would come in at all times of the day, and in between you had to fit in your cleaning.

I just accepted whatever came along. Every stage you get into something, and I just adjusted to whatever was before me. Two sons and two daughters. Oh yes, it was hard. We didn't have nannies in those days. You'd have to take care of the family, take care of the business — and my husband was an alderman. As his wife, I was sometimes called to open bazaars when the mayor's wife couldn't. So I found that I was really on the go.

DR. LINDA LEE

During my internship, I went up to Sioux Lookout in Northern Ontario and worked on an Indian reserve for a month. There was no electricity or running water. I was all by myself with all this dental equipment that I had to put together (laugh). I was just hopeless. But I got one of the Indian guys to help.... It was such a remote community, they'd never seen a Chinese person before, so they didn't know what I was. But after I told them I was Chinese, we became very friendly. We could tell whiteman jokes. They liked me and I got lots of work done.

I had such a good time that the next year I went up to Inuvik, in the Arctic, for a month. Again, I had a great time seeing parts of the country that I would never have had an opportunity to see. It was also a good experience because I was doing something worthwhile. In Toronto, you get very tired of telling people to floss their teeth — because you know they're not going to do it. You go up there, and you pull out fifty teeth in one day — or you do twenty fillings. You're really helping these people. I was the only dentist in the whole McKenzie Delta. People were chartering planes to come because they heard there was a dentist in the area. You really feel worthwhile. It gives you some perspective. So when I came back to the city, I didn't take it all too seriously — you know, dentistry, flossing your teeth — realizing that other people have it much worse. When I was released from my job, I went back up north for the summer and worked on a whole bunch of Indian reserves in Ontario....

After getting my Masters in Pathology in the States, I heard they needed an oral pathologist in Saskatchewan. I got the job — which was good, because there are no other jobs in Canada (laugh).... Oh yes, I enjoy my work. I like the teaching too, because I feel I'm making an impact. I think I'm doing a pretty good job — and that makes me feel good.

No, I don't feel I'm treated differently as a Chinese. I'm the only woman they've ever hired at the school, so it's more that I'm a woman than that I'm Chinese (laugh). I always tease them. There is one Japanese guy who said, "We've never had anyone like you here before." And I said, "What do you mean — short?" (laugh) He didn't even get it. I don't think anyone sees me as being Chinese at all. I don't get singled out for that.

The support staff — secretaries, dental assistants, nurses — are all women, right? They've never had to answer to a woman before. So I think I tend to do a lot more of my own typing. I do my own clean up — and I make my own coffee. I think (laugh) ... if I were a man, I wouldn't have to do all those things. But I do those things deliberately because I know these women are already jealous. I know they say things to me that they would never say to any of the men. Well, for example, I don't wear jewelry, except sometimes these earcuffs, since I don't have pierced ears. Well, the head of one of the departments is a man who wears a diamond earring — no one ever says anything to him. But to me, the girls say, "What's that thing you've got on your ear?" "How come you wear your dresses so long?" You know, that type of thing, whereas I'm sure they would never question a man about his appearance.

The other thing is that I'm single, and there are very few other single people — except the secretaries and assistants, so I'm direct competition for them. Then there are a couple of men in maintenance and supplies who give me a really hard time. They've never had to answer to a woman before. You know, I come along and ask for something, and they'll say, "What for?" Well, wait a second, you wouldn't say that to one of the guys. But that's how they treat me — and I accept that. That's just the way it is (laugh).

In dental school in Toronto, the teachers were very old and very British. They'd say, "Oh look dear, let me show you how to do that. You can't do this." And I'd just get really mad and say, "Let me try first!" I think part of that made me work harder. You have to be better than the guys just to break even. And that's the way I've always been.

This field is such a man's world that they don't know how to react to a woman. And so I tease them. I give it right back to them. One guy came up to me and said, "Well Linda, you're never going to make it in Saskatchewan unless you curl and golf. You're never going to get tenure." Then I said, "I don't care about tenure — I'm just waiting for a rich man (laugh)." He didn't know what to say next, wondering, "Does she really mean this?" I let them think that I'm cavalier about my career — even though I obviously can't be if I'm where I am now. I've worked hard for it.

Notes

1. Freemasons — the Chinese Freemasons — one of the earliest Chinese social organizations in Canada, established in 1876 and known as the *Cheekungtang* (CKT). It was considered a "secret society" because the CKT opposed the Manchu ruled Qing Dynasty.

2. Chinese Benevolent Association (C.B.A.) — a mutual aid association established by Chinese merchants in Victoria and inaugurated in 1884 as the Chinese Consolidated Benevolent Association. Its early initiatives focussed on campaigning against discriminatory legislation and social problems facing the many Chinese left unemployed after the completion of the CPR.

CHINATOWN VIGNETTES

SANDRA LEE

In the following excerpt, Sandra describes scenes from the past as told to her by her mother, Mae.

There were actually a lot of Chinese men in the town Union Bay — men with families back in China or Hong Kong. So all these Chinese men in the village bought everything from the store my grandfather had. They spent a lot of time there. The store became like a smokehouse or gathering place. Mom, being the oldest daughter, they all spent time with her. They looked after her — taught her things, told her stories.

These men worked as trimmers. They went down to the ships and filled them with coal from the Cumberland mines, brought down by train, right to the wharf.[1] They filled up the bunkers, one after another, until there was enough coal for the ship to return to Japan. We'd see that every day. You don't see that anymore.

MARY WONG

Well if a restaurant had to hire somebody, they always went to Toronto to get a cook, because there was nobody sitting around Hamilton waiting to get a job. So people moved in from other places. Well I think the Chinese community had a sense of community in those days. There were only a few of us then — but we stuck together. Oh yes, when we went to Chinese school, we had the Chinese Sunday school picnic. There was a group of us, maybe seventy-five or a hundred. We managed to get together — and somebody had *guat how, muan yet*, shaving the baby's head after his first month, and stuff like that. And everybody would make *tai* and bring the *doong*, the sticky rice wrapped in palm leaves — and pass it around. They don't do so much of that with Canadians, but the Chinese people believe that whatever you make, you should give some to your friends. My mother used to tell me to take the *tai* she made over to Annie's parents. Then maybe the next day, they would bring us some of what they made.

VALERIE MAH

It was a big thing to come to Toronto when I was small because we'd drive up to Toronto as a family when we could get away. I can remember going down into Chinatown and going to the theatre with my dad. We'd watch the Chinese opera, seeing people pushing chairs around that were pretend lions. We used to come to Toronto to go to the Santa Claus parade, and we'd visit my uncle, Henry Lore, at 109 Dundas Street. Then we'd stay at the Ford Hotel which was on the corner of Bay and Dundas where the Atrium is now. It was a big thing to go to Toronto.

LIL LEE

In those days, even if my mother had wanted to work, it was impossible for a woman to find a job — unless she wanted to be, say, a waitress in one of those Chinese restaurants (laugh), or one of those, umm ... Chinese women who sort of hung around the gambling places (laugh). They had little pet names for all these women. This one woman was quite ugly, and they would say her face was like a locomotive and call her *Chia-hau, ah* (laugh).[2] I imagine they were quite young. When we went to Chinatown, we'd see these ladies of the night, or whatever you call them, standing by the doorways smoking. In those days, it was quite unusual to see a woman smoke. I didn't notice any housewives smoking cigarettes. But these women would be accompanying the men, you know, gambling or whatever. I don't know whether they were prostitutes. They may have been.

SHIRLEY WELSH

My dad and my grandfather — they both owned restaurants. My grandfather came to Canada in 1912. He was in Flin Flon, Manitoba. He had a restaurant there — he didn't like it up there. Then he went to so many places, finally settling down in Swift

Current, Saskatchewan. He had about ten partners in this one restaurant. John Diefenbaker used to go there for supper — he wasn't Prime Minister then. But I remember because my grandfather always made a point of saying, "This is Mr. so and so..." I thought, "big deal" (laugh). I also remember Tommy Douglas, the first leader of the NDP (CCF). That restaurant was getting the most business in town. I remember they used to line up way outside of the restaurant trying to get in (laugh).

Instead of buying a house in Swift Current, my grandfather rented the upstairs of a grocery store. The grocery business had nothing to do with my family at all, but it was only across the street and into the alley to my grandfather's restaurant — that's how close we were. Then the sons and cousins went and set up another restaurant, just down a few blocks from the father's and uncle's. My dad and his cousins called it Mandarin. But it didn't do well. Also, it burnt down. From then on, the families went to small towns to start their own businesses. Small towns because there was less competition. Also, I found that people just enjoyed Chinese food. If you travel to every one of those small towns, you'll find there's always a Chinese restaurant (laugh).

GRACE LEE

When I was a child, there was this very rich Chinese man who invited only the Chinese to dinner in his garden at his home once a year. Those were very happy occasions. His daughter still lives here. In those days, there were a few very rich Chinese here. Some of their descendants still live here. The rich women were very grand. Whenever they were invited out for dinner, they would wrap their beautiful clothes in a bundle and change when they got to their destination. Then they would change back into their street clothes when they left. It was very grand! Even the children had to change clothes. This man used to send a *kuan yin* carriage to pick us up. This was a horse drawn carriage driven by someone called Ah-Jack. He always used to drive the rich people around.

Nowadays, if you are invited out you are sent an invitation card. If you want to attend, you just go on that day. But in those days, the host would first send a servant to deliver the invitation to your house. Then the servant would return later to see if you were really going. Finally, he would come to pick you up personally. We were treated like very precious people....

The rich Chinese here numbered about ten families. They were all business people. My father opened Wing Tung Yuen, a grocery store. Later we were the first to open a place that manufactured green houses. In those days, the Chinese operated only groceries, greenhouses, restaurants and laundries.

JEAN LEE

In Windsor there were several restaurants: ours, my husband's parents' — and then a few run by single Chinese men. So there were quite a few spotted around the city. The Chinese community in Windsor at that time didn't have too much in the way of activities. They did have the Chinese Benevolent Association, where the men go for their meetings ... and once in a while they had a tea party. But that was about it.

The women didn't have anything. At first there was my mother and my husband Eddy's mother. When a couple more families moved in, then they got together and made, you know, *tai* — Chinese pastries and stuff. They'd go to each other's houses, and that was their main social life. They didn't really get together much. Eventually, there were about four or five families in Windsor, and they all had restaurants — they all had to work...

When we were real young, we used to go once in a while to watch Chinese theatre. After the play they'd serve oranges and pastries. That's the social life we used to have. I didn't understand the play (laugh). My parents liked it, but I remember there were men pretending to be women. I could tell because the actors came out and ate afterwards.

Eddy's family's restaurant was called King's Cafe. In 1913 this girl's mother went to the restaurant with a bunch of guys. They were all drinking and they got sort of drunk. She saw this teapot and said, "Is that ever a beautiful teapot. I really like it." When they left and got into their car, one of the guys said, "Here, I got something for you." He handed her the teapot filled with tea. His pants were all wet. "Here, I swiped you a teapot." And so, she kept it and kept it — until 1978, just before she died. She called her daughter and told her the whole story of how she got this teapot. She said, "It belongs to a family by the name of King Lee in the King's Cafe. I want you to return it to their family." And so on November 30th, 1978, this daughter called Eddy and asked him if he was King Lee's son. She told him the story about her mother, having this teapot — and how she felt so guilty about it all these years and that it should go back to its rightful owner before she died, so she could die peacefully. So that's how he got it. This woman got it in 1913 — and her daughter gave it back to us on November 30th, 1978. That was her last request…to return this teapot back to the Lee family. The teapot is an antique. And it came from China.

Notes

1. Cumberland mines — a coal mining community on Vancouver Island which had a substantial Chinese population.
2. Lil Lee's reference to Chinese prostitutes. *Chia-hau, ah* is Toisan slang meaning, "hey, locomotive head."

HOW COME YOU DON'T HAVE AN ACCENT?

ANNE FONG

You know how, as children, you want to be like everybody else —
and yet, you can't be, because you're a visible minority? And you
know that you always will be a visible minority. So then you have
that conflict within yourself, that you wish you weren't Chinese.
You wish you were one of the *lo fan*. It was very hard for those of
us in the first generation born here. We had to come to terms with
ourselves about that inner conflict. I think it's really kind of a
lifetime struggle.

It wasn't until I was in my thirties that I got over that phase. I
would really be bugged when people would say, "Are you
Chinese or Japanese?" And I'd think, "I'm Canadian. I was born
here!" They would say, "You? How can you be Canadian?" Then
I'd say, "Well, you don't even know the definition of *Canadian*.
Canadian means anybody born in this country, you know." Later
on, my answer to their question would be, "Chinese Canadian,"
because I knew they wanted to know where you're from. Then I
would add that my parents came from China. But still, even in the
1960s, people would say: "How come you don't have an accent?"

I knew that my children would have to work out this identity
conflict themselves, but I wanted them to be proud of their
Chinese heritage at the same time — of their two heritages. For a
while, my nineteen year old daughter did not want anything
Chinese. But now she's very interested in learning both Cantonese
and Mandarin. And she realizes that to know yourself, you really
have to know where you came from. You have to understand your
past first.

My own personal interests are more Canadian and European
than Chinese. Just because you're Chinese, doesn't mean you're
going to be immensely interested in the culture. Everybody is
different. It was very important to me that my children have a

background in European music, art and literature. I never thought much about sending them to Chinese school, but I felt they should have some involvement in it, since Chinese is their heritage. You're really all the richer for it because you have another culture to draw from. And you're not a plain, ordinary Canadian.

I remember a lot of racial discrimination. The taunts they'd yell at you: "Chinky, chinky Chinaman, sitting on the fence, trying to make a dollar out of fifty cents." People would make fun of our chopsticks and the smells of our cooking. I always remember feeling ashamed whenever I had a Canadian friend over. My mother would hang out this *bok choy* from her garden to dry out for the winter. And people would make fun of that too. You know, "Oh, look at that! Yuk! Look at that stuff they eat!"

In those days, we weren't even considered human. People would say things like, "All you Chinese, you got pig eyes, pig noses, pig mouths." We really had it rubbed into us that we were inferior. It takes a lot to overcome that. Maybe it's overcome with your own accomplishments, thinking it over and understanding human nature more — why people do the things they do. It's insecurity in themselves when they have to put down others. When you understand that, then you don't feel angry or hurt.

LINDA LEE

My Chinese heritage is very important to me. And I think I'm more aware of it since my mother passed away and I have children of my own. I think all the years that I was growing up, I wasn't terribly aware of being Chinese. I don't think I was overly conscious of it. But now that my mother isn't here, the connection has gone. So I'm trying to re-establish the connection myself, partly for me and partly for my children....

I think it has to do with history and background. We're a visible minority — I mean it's obvious that I'm Chinese. My kids, who I often think look a fair bit Chinese, don't look Chinese at all next to completely Chinese kids (laugh). But it's obvious that their background is not entirely Anglo-Saxon. And I think they need to know from whence all of this came.

VELMA CHAN

We didn't pass on any Chinese values to our children. We have a general cosmopolitan outlook. I find a lot of Hong Kong people still carry on the old traditions and rituals, like setting up their gods and ancestral tablets. Some of our cousins are still burning their *joss sticks* every month in front of their dead relatives. Then their children don't follow the old ways. I believe in bending with the tide, going along with the Canadian ways.

I'd call myself a typical Chinese Canadian woman, which is pretty hard to define. I think a woman has to maintain her own identity by being independent. The education here certainly broadens your horizons, so that a woman can better maintain her position. I think it's up to the Chinese Canadian woman to strive to be a regular Canadian.

I met a lot of Chinese people in Vancouver before I got married. Chinese Canadians of my generation were all evolving, becoming Canadianized. There must have been conflict with the older Chinese generation. I know that some of the older families thought that any job that a woman was doing was just a stop-gap before settling down. But my friends and I were rebels. We wanted to further our education and choose our own husbands.

MARY WONG

I had friends who were Irish and Scottish. We used to play hopscotch, skipping and hide and seek on the streets, or go for walks. I never went inside their houses. I'd just call their names out whenever I passed by. No one told me that I had to do this. I just automatically knew I had to call them from outside because I was Chinese. Nobody had to tell you that you were Chinese. You just knew that you were different. When you're the only Chinese person at school, you sort of try to behave all the time. Definitely, at a very early age you learned that you had to follow a certain code of behaviour.

Later when I started in business, I'd say to the help, "Do not speak Chinese in front of Canadians." It was a real no-no in those days. But nowadays it's more accepted. People are encouraged to be themselves and keep their cultures, which I think is a good idea. When the multiculturalism policy was introduced in 1971, I was on the council. I found it very interesting.... This policy has certainly made Canada a more interesting country.

FRANCIS WONG

Chinese friends? Well, there was Gretta's family and that was it. Oh gosh, there were under a dozen families in Ontario in those days. There were quite a few single men though. Gretta's family was very different from mine. Her father was very modern. The Chinese community used to say that he had "gone Canadian." They didn't like that. He'd go to church, eat Canadian food, read their newspapers. He just fit in with the Canadians, shaking their hands and patting them on the back, just like a Westerner would do. But later on, I think all the Chinese families changed too — maybe not the parents, but definitely the children. We are definitely more Canadianized.

I wouldn't say I've had any bad racial experiences. But once, after I got married, Gretta and I went into this silk store in Toronto's Chinatown. Two ladies were behind the counter. One was talking very loud, and for a long time. I asked her in English, "How much is that blouse in the window?" She replied, "Are you Chinese?" I said, "Yes." She said, "How come you don't speak Chinese?" I said, "You never asked me." And she said, "So what?" I said, "Well, if you're in Canada, you'd better speak Canadian." Again, she said, "So what? Most of time I don't even answer anybody Chinese who speaks to me in English." It took me all night to get over that incident. What bothered me most was that this woman would not speak to me just because I didn't speak Chinese.

MARY MOHAMMED

The only time that I really felt I was different was when I was being called names by some of my schoolmates. I wondered why they were being so mean. I remember one case where this friendly little girl took me to her house and her parents slammed the door in my face. And then she could no longer be my friend. Just because I was Chinese. My friend couldn't understand why her mother wouldn't let her play with me.

I remember it was a very bad time for being Chinese when the Canadians were all against the Japanese in the Second World War. Some people would just look at you and start calling you "Jap." My friends wouldn't call me that. It was the people going by on the street. No, it wasn't an easy time for anyone who looked different.

I would say that the earlier years were difficult because there weren't many Chinese in Halifax, but then the community grew and people realized that we were really harmless. We became more or less accepted.

I know that when my older sons were growing up, they still got teased a lot about being Chinese. They used to come home crying, "We're Canadians, but they're calling us 'Chinks.'" They were very upset and wished that they hadn't been born Chinese. But I don't think they get that racist taunting now.

WINNIE NG

Winnie was born in Hong Kong in 1951. She came to Canada in 1968. She currently resides in Toronto.

When my daughter, Claire, was about three years old, she came with a picture of herself with blond hair. I remember I got kind of upset, questioning her — "what colour is your hair?" (laugh) I figured no matter how much you want to assimilate, there are people who say, "As long as you treat people well, you'll be reciprocated." But I don't think I believe that anymore. As a non-white Canadian, as a Chinese Canadian, you need to assert yourself.

For me, the whole identification of myself as a "Canadian" has been a very gradual process. I came here in 1968. When I was a student, I saw myself as a "student." I didn't see myself as part of the Chinese Canadian community. But once you get involved in working in the community, eventually there's a process of moving from identifying yourself as an immigrant to identifying yourself as a Canadian of Chinese origin. Having two children here sort of prompted that process — and the fact that those labels, at a certain point, are arbitrary.

JANE WOO

I learned a lot about Chinese customs and etiquette from my older sister who came over from China. These were practices that were taught to her, although perhaps they don't even bother doing these things now in China. Things like: never starting to eat until your elders start, never banging your chopsticks or digging into the food from the other side of the plate. We were taught to respect our elders, to be hospitable. These values exist in all cultures, of course. But they seem to be more so in the Chinese ways. If you entered a Chinese home, you couldn't address everyone by their first names. You have to acknowledge their relationship to you as *suk* or *hsien seng* — or *bak.*

VALERIE MAH

There were only two Chinese families in Brockville, so most of our friends were Canadian. As very, very young children we spoke Chinese. We talked to the cooks in our restaurant in Chinese.

But we mostly spoke English at home. We were basically raised Canadian. But each year we had to leave school in May and go to the cemetery for *Ching Ming,* decoration day. At first we were a little embarrassed. Who would want people to know that you left school to have a picnic in the cemetery? We decorated and put food on the graves and planted flowers in remembrance and respect of our ancestors. The whole Chinese community of about twenty-five in Brockville would go together. My dad was sort of the leader of the community. He'd shoot his pistol to ward off evil spirits and we'd pour liquor on the graves.

I've never felt that I've missed something because I was born Chinese. The only time I've ever had any discrimination was on my sixth or seventh birthday when we took all my little friends skating. Some older boys started calling my brother and me, "Chinky, Chinky, Chinaman," and all of us, including my

Canadian friends, went home crying to my mother. My mother just said, "They're ignorant, so don't pay attention to them." After that, I've never felt discriminated against. I've always felt that being Chinese is an asset to me. In fact, I was hired by a principal who said, "Chinese are hard workers, so that's why I want you."

MAY CHOW

I haven't experienced too much discrimination because of my difficulty communicating in English. But I do feel that some Westerners don't want Chinese people as friends. There were times when my children were being laughed at just for being Chinese. Sometimes they'd come home and talk about having fights at school. When my second son was in grade five, he wouldn't speak Chinese, because he said being Chinese was shameful. Then in grade eight, he started to learn French, and I told him that learning French was like learning Chinese. If you don't speak it, you won't really learn it. You'll forget it. So after that he started speaking Chinese again.

I don't really follow Chinese customs. The elders are not here, so we do nothing religious at home. We have rice every night, and the children know their Chinese names and numbers, but they've had no opportunity to go to Chinese schools. I speak Toisanese to them most of the time, and they answer me in English.

LILY WELSH

Lily was born in China in 1950. She immigrated to Canada in 1951. At the time of her interview, she was residing in Edmonton.

I don't think my daughter is conscious about being Chinese. When she was a lot younger, she used to say, "I'm part Chinese and part white." I mean, I taught her that she's part Chinese and part white. So she would go to school and she'd tell other people. The other day she came home and told me she was walking home with a Chinese girl. Our daughter told this other girl that she was part Chinese and part white. The other girl, who is completely Chinese, told my daughter that *she* herself is also part Chinese and part white.

Actually, I was very conscious of being Chinese myself. In Unity, Saskatchewan, where I grew up, I knew that there were quite a few boys who liked me, but I was very shy and never did talk to them. I noticed that they just kept on looking at me. I always felt too shy to even say hi to the guys. I was always worried about what other people would think. What would other white people say if they saw me going out on a date with a white guy? I always felt kind of self-conscious in that area.

I usually use the word, "Chinese Canadian." When I say "Canadian," I guess I think only about the white people — although I am actually a Canadian myself. I also use the term "Chinese," because, after all, I am a Chinese person. But because I grew up in Canada, I most often call myself a "Chinese Canadian." I don't really think about Chinese culture much because my parents didn't follow the customs that thoroughly. My dad was too busy working and he more or less grew up here.

I don't think I'm a typical Chinese Canadian woman. I feel like I'm in between. To me, a typical Chinese Canadian woman is one who is so westernized that she follows everything the white person's way. And I don't feel that I'm like that because I know a lot of the Chinese customs and I do mingle with a lot of Chinese people. As a matter of fact, I have a lot of girlfriends who are Chinese, but Canadian raised. But maybe I really think of a Chinese Canadian as someone who thinks she's ... white. I've met some like that.

I have not always felt proud to be Chinese. Sometimes I too have wished I was white (laugh), so I could be in the majority instead of being in the minority. I suppose I feel that way when I get depressed. I don't resent white people. I realize that even among the white people there are all different kinds. Even though I'm in the minority, I have gotten over the feelings I had when I was younger, worrying all the time about people not liking me because I'm Chinese. It's only when you get older that you understand that sometimes what people think about you is not as important as what you think of yourself. You also understand that people accept you for what you are, really. But sometimes, if they don't like you, it still makes you feel like you're so alone.

When I came out to the city, I got along very well with the Chinese people I met. If I made mistakes in speaking Chinese, I never felt bad. I could be excused because I grew up in Canada. But if I made a mistake speaking English, I felt really bad. I really put myself down.

Sometimes I feel very inadequate in my English. Maybe it's because I went through so many years of being very quiet. I find that that's the case with a lot of Chinese. When you're in a minority, you feel different. And when you feel different, you feel kind of inadequate. It's only when you get older that you realize how silly that thinking is. But then, the thing is that when you go through life being so quiet, that quietness becomes a part of you.

TAM GOOSEN

I always felt sympathetic to the identity problems of Canadian-born Chinese. I remember being very upset when I first came here and I went to a party. Somebody — he was white — asked me where I was from. When I said, "Hong Kong," he replied, "You're not Chinese!" I got mad and confronted this person. "What do you mean, only Chinese from Communist China are true Chinese?" You can extend the question further. Is a Chinese born here even *less* Chinese? Are the Hong Kong Chinese less Chinese than those from Taiwan? This whole business about Chineseness is very silly. How do you define it?

It has to do with your own individual self-identification. I don't have the perfect answer. I mean what about a person like my husband, Ted, who has immersed himself in Chinese culture through his academic studies? Some of my friends consider him an honorary Chinese. In a sense, I have a lot of sympathy for Canadian-born Chinese who can't speak Cantonese — or for the Hong Kong Chinese who can't speak Mandarin.

DR. LINDA LEE

For some reason we didn't learn Chinese, so we became very

defensive about it. We didn't have any Chinese friends. In fact, we lived in Cabbagetown. It was mostly Italian and French Canadian, very lower class immigrant, but not too many Chinese. I remember when we'd go down to Chinatown on Sundays with my dad, people would laugh at us because we couldn't speak Chinese. The assumption was that if you looked Chinese, you should be able to speak Chinese. There's no excuse. Then if you can't, it's as if you're a traitor. Chinese people would actually point and laugh at us! So of course, we weren't going to make friends with any of them.

Later at university, I found that I didn't have much in common with other Chinese students. When I was in first year physics, it was mostly Chinese and Jewish kids, and the instructor was Chinese. He could barely speak English. Before I even opened my mouth, he came up to me and said, "You were born here, weren't you?" — just like that. And I said, "How did you know?" He said, "I can tell by the way you act, and the way you dress" — as if it was completely disgusting that I was behaving like a Canadian. The Chinese here from China are very quiet, unassuming. They sort of do their job and go home and don't make any waves. I'm not like that.

When I was interning at Toronto Western Hospital, a Chinese patient came in. He couldn't speak English, but when he saw me he thought, oh great, no problem. But when I had to go get an interpreter for him, he pointed and said, *"Lo fan!"* I didn't have much exposure to Chinese people. Actually, I stayed away from them because I felt they thought I was inferior. I didn't want to have to go through explaining why I couldn't speak Chinese.

One funny thing about all overseas Orientals is the way they can come up to you and say, "What are you?" It happens to me all the time. I know that they're curious, but it's very rude. It shouldn't make any difference what I am. If they want to know about my ethnic background, that's something else, but when they say so bluntly, "What are you," I feel like replying, "I'm a person." The Caucasians don't seem to be concerned about my ethnicity. We all look alike. They just assume I'm Chinese.

CAROLINE CHAN

I don't feel Chinese and I don't feel Canadian. I went to China to live for six months as an English teacher. One of the reasons I went to China was to see what it was like. I wanted to see where my family came from. I wanted to understand some of the traditions we observed at home. When I got there, I was treated like I didn't belong — like I was a foreigner. The Chinese treated me like I was a Canadian, but they didn't want me to have the same freedom and liberal treatment as a non-Chinese Canadian. So they saw me as a Chinese but not a Chinese. But here in Canada people don't think of me as a Canadian. They look upon me first as a Chinese. When I was in school, I remember it was really hard for me to make friends because I felt that prejudicial barrier, that cultural difference. It was really strong. As a matter of fact, there were times when people would point to me and say, "Oh, you don't want to play with her, she's Chinese." This happened a lot in my earlier years, from grades one to six.

FERN HUM

There is a cultural gap between the Canadian-born Chinese and the overseas Chinese. We used to call them CBCs — China-born Chinese (laugh). And I guess people from Hong Kong called us CBCs too — Canadian-born Chinese. I got to know a small circle of Canadian-born through my brother. He met them through his association at Queen's University in Kingston. He also got to know some here in Toronto, people like Jean Lumb and her kids. We had this common thing — we didn't know the Chinese language well enough to associate ourselves with the overseas Chinese.

We didn't think that the overseas Chinese really understood our feelings about not understanding the language and culture. They didn't understand the dilemma we had to face. You know, we're brought up in a Western society where we assimilated so well that we're almost like Anglo-Canadians, yet we know that we have Chinese faces. We have yellow skin and slanted eyes, yet we're not accepted by many of the overseas Chinese. So we felt isolated, not belonging to either group. We don't look Anglo — and we don't speak Chinese. Without the language, you lose so much of the culture.... We were left out in the middle.

When I was going to Ryerson in Toronto, my husband introduced me to an association of Canadian-born Chinese. I sort of felt at home with people in this association because everyone spoke English (laugh). We sort of had similar ambivalent feelings. Later on, my brother introduced me to more Canadian-born and there were conferences for us to talk about our shared experiences.

My Chinese is so bad. I can understand more than I can converse. If we're in the nursery at the church which has a seventy-five percent Chinese congregation, I can understand the teachers when they're talking in Chinese, but I usually respond in English (laugh) — which is terrible.

I want so badly to be able to converse in Chinese and be accepted as a Chinese person. I guess I feel that if I'm Chinese, I should *speak* Chinese. That's another thing that I'm trying to instill in my three-year-old — "If you're Chinese, you have to — you should speak Chinese." It's what my parents always taught me although they really didn't adhere to it. Now I feel embarrassed if I respond to a Chinese person in English. If people are already having a conversation in Chinese, I just don't think it's right for me to start conversing with them in English. It would be a funny dialogue with one side in Chinese and the other side in English.

My husband, Doug, says that Canadian-born are like bananas: yellow on the outside and white inside. I think this is partly true. We have so many white attitudes and values, but our skin is yellow. There was this white guy from a missionary family who was in China for quite some time, so their kids grew up in a Chinese culture. This fellow spoke Chinese quite well, better than Doug did. And he said to Doug one day, "Gee Doug, you're not Chinese. You just look it on the outside." Actually, Doug's Chinese is a lot better than mine. He can speak Cantonese surprisingly well for a Canadian-born, but he can't read or write Chinese.... No, I'm not offended by the term "banana." It's an accurate description. Have you ever heard the term, *juk sing*, hollow bamboo? I never really understood it until somebody explained it to me and I said, "Gee, that's not very nice. But it's true."

It's funny that the Canadian-born are the ones more interested in preserving and understanding the Chinese culture. But we find it so difficult to really get to know the culture because we can't read Chinese. We can only find out about it through our parents, through listening to them — and through English language sources. And then, it's not completely true.

IRENE CHU

The most blatant incident of discrimination I suffered was in Montreal in 1963. I had just arrived from Hong Kong. My husband-to-be lived across the street from a French Catholic church. I attended daily mass there and naturally assumed it would be no problem to be married there. We were astounded to be told that we could not get married there. The priest said, "You're not French, you are Chinese. Go back to your Chinese church. We don't look after you."

The irony of the episode was that a few months down the road the same priest came knocking on our door asking for donations. It appeared he did not mind taking money from the Chinese, but to provide service to one was certainly out of the question.

I don't believe in bringing up my children in the Catholic faith. After I came to Canada I became totally disillusioned about the Catholic Church.

It's far better to live by one's own principles. This is the primary difference between Western culture and Chinese moral values. The Western value system depends too much on Christian faith, on the theory of heaven and hell after life. When the religious belief falters, there goes the entire value system and moral conviction. Western religions, predominantly Catholicism and Christianity, are dictatorial in nature. They don't allow liberalism. The Chinese are traditionally very liberal in their worship. They call upon their ancestors, they supplicate all deities who have any reputation for being benevolent. The Chinese do not impose the supernatural onto their value system to keep it in place.

I don't agree with many aspects of Confucianism. Confucius' teaching imposes too many restrictions and limitations. The essence of Chinese traditions and culture is contained in the written material. Despite attempts in the past of total destruction of written knowledge, books and recorded history remain the backbone of our culture.

RAMONA MAR

In my second year of university I really started thinking about things like feminism and what it meant to be Chinese Canadian. I would have gone out of my way to make friends with other Chinese Canadians since there were no other Chinese Canadians at my high school. But you see a lot of Chinese at university. The Hong Kong kids seem to congregate into one big gang in the library. Then you'd see the Chinese Canadian kids looking pretty hip and mainstream. The two groups did not hang around together. Then I guess there was the odd one like me who just floated.

In the summer of 1979 I went on a student trip to Taiwan. That was a turning point in my life. The trip was for North American-born Chinese, sponsored by the Taiwanese government. They brought three hundred of us over to Taipei and opened their arms to us, saying, "Welcome to the homeland!" We all knew that it was a propaganda tour, but we just ignored the politics. I was surrounded by young people like me. Most of them didn't speak Cantonese or Mandarin. They all had parents who wanted them to be high achievers.

Soon after I returned from Taiwan, the W5 controversy was heating up and I got involved as a member of the Chinese Benevolent Society's Ad Hoc Committee. It was all new and exciting to me because I was meeting people my own age who were interested in doing something for the community. I met some people who were part of a radio collective called Pender Guy, named after the main street in Vancouver's Chinatown. Before I knew it, I became part of the collective. They were articulating my own sense of the world, exploring subjects like the W5 controversy, immigration — even what it was like to be a "banana," you know, white on the inside, yellow on the outside. What made the radio show even more unique for me was that it was in English. It identified something I had yet to label: Chinese Canadian culture. It is not solely Chinese, nor is it white Canadian. Our culture is a blend of both.

The Pender Guy experience helped me to recognize Chinese Canadian culture, that we have a history right here in this country: the railroad, the Head Tax, the Exclusion Act. Chinese Canadian culture is something entirely different from Chinese culture. Even though I feel thoroughly Canadian, the rest of society doesn't see it that way. The W5 incident got me sensitive enough to realize that when I walk down the street, people don't say, "Her family's been here for generations." They say, "There's a Chinese woman." They don't say "Chinese Canadian." The assumption is that I'm an immigrant, that I don't belong here — and that being a Canadian means being a *white* Canadian.

Now I no longer feel uncomfortable with overseas Chinese. I think the Taiwan trip and visiting my cousins in Hong Kong changed that. I met people from all kinds of backgrounds ... Chinese Americans, Taiwan Chinese. I understand a lot more now. The W5 Committee also exposed me to many other Chinese Canadians who'd come from overseas, and we all worked successfully together toward a common goal.

Working in the media has attuned me to media stereotypes. We may have progressed a bit from the "Charlie Chan" and "China Doll" images, but they've been replaced by other stereotypes. Every time a story comes up about a Chinatown gang, people have visions of knives in the streets and heroin addicts ripping up gambling joints. We need to have correct images of ourselves but that means that we have to be more vigilant monitoring the images which appear, or more often than not, the images which do not appear. Also, I think we all need to see ourselves in non-traditional roles. We might still run restaurants, laundromats and corners stores, but we should also see ourselves as politicians, scholars, firefighters, and so on.

SHIRLEY WELSH

My Chinese background does not affect me very much. Even though I was born in China, it's like I was really born here. I think perhaps because I came here so young and I was educated here.

I've never gone through an identity crisis. Sometimes I wish that I had gone through it. I wish I had remembered myself as being Chinese (laugh). There are so many times when I'm just not self-conscious of it. I guess my heart says that's the way to be. Don't feel self-conscious about being Chinese — just be as you are.

NO GOOD-NIGHT
KISS — NO TALK!

DR. LINDA LEE

By the time I started living with a Caucasian boyfriend, my mother had gotten tired of fighting about it. Only two sisters married Chinese while the rest married Caucasians. Mother used to be very bad. I remember when I was a little kid, she'd sit on the porch with the butcher knife if my sister was out with a Caucasian guy (laugh). She'd just sit there with that knife and say, "Okay, you go home now! No goodnight kiss, no talk!" (laugh) She would just scare them away. But if the guy was Chinese, there'd be no problem. So we didn't bring guys home much (laugh).

Sure, I want to get married, sure ... but I've never been at the right place at the right time, I guess. Actually, with one of my relationships, a major problem was that I'm Chinese and his parents didn't like that. But I'm glad that it didn't work out (laugh), because I was holding back on my career. Then I went into graduate school which, of course, limits me again. Now I can only go to major centres where there's a dental school.

My boyfriend lives in Toronto, so that's kind of hard. But there's no job for me there. We don't know what's going to happen with our relationship. We don't know if it's serious enough for me to leave. He was offered a job here, but he decided not to take it because he didn't want me to take the responsibility of him being unhappy if he didn't like it here.

I think I still want to get married and have kids, but I just can't plan that. What happens, happens. It's more important for me to be happy doing what I'm doing rather than being married and unhappy. So right now I'm just ... waiting (laugh), I guess.

BETTY TOY

Betty was born in Windsor, Ontario in 1956. At the time of her interview, she was residing in Windsor.

I didn't really go out with many overseas Chinese guys. You just didn't have enough in common to go out with each other. Well for example, once my aunt tried to set me up with her Chinese neighbour's son. This guy was impossible! I couldn't stand him (laugh). No life to him at all. And he played games too. He'll hide what he really thinks and tell you something else. I like people who are honest. He asked me if I wanted a drink — meaning alcoholic drink. I was going to say yes, but then I thought, I don't know this guy, so I said, "No thank you." And he said, "Good, because I was just asking you to test you." Then he said that he didn't like girls who smoke or wear make-up. A lot of nerve, eh? He was very old-fashioned. I just couldn't handle it.

One Canadian guy I went out with briefly told me he had never gone out with a Chinese girl before. That's why he went out with me. I felt very, very offended when he said that because he wasn't relating to me as a person. He didn't like *me*. He was just interested in dating a, quote, "Chinese girl." I have nothing against interracial marriage. There are certain problems involved, depending on how other people view it. But personally, if I were to marry a Canadian guy, that guy would have to respect Chinese culture and try to understand it — not look down upon it. This one guy I went out with actually said to me, "My mother likes you more than my dad does. She's willing to overlook the fact that you're Chinese." Can you believe that?

VICTORIA YIP

I got married when I was twenty. In a way, it was an arranged marriage, but in a way it was not. My cousin introduced us. My cousin and husband belonged to the same Chinese student soccer team. Actually, my husband was quite well known as a soccer player at that time....

My marriage is quite happy — very happy. Yes, we share in

the decision making. Well, he leaves all the home things — furniture or whatever I want to buy — he leaves it to me. But the big decisions — education or buying a car or house, that's his decision.

MARY MOHAMMED

Oh, it was just terrible after I started to go with Mo, my husband, you know — just because he was Indian. They thought it was a disgrace. The Chinese community had an official meeting with my parents. They said that what I was doing was a disgrace to the Chinese community. And of course, my parents reacted to that. They felt very badly, I mean, to begin with, it was hard on them because they wanted me to marry Chinese. So it was very traumatic. I was in my early twenties. I felt I was old enough (laugh).

The Chinese community continued to object to my marriage for almost fifteen or twenty years. And it hurt me so much. Because we were the second Chinese family here, we got to know all the newcomers. My mom and I would help them get settled. Then when they turned against me, they weren't very nice to my mom. And it hurt me so much, so I just stayed away. My husband and I moved away because he was studying. We lived in Winnipeg and then B.C. But we came back to Halifax. I feel this is my home.

You know, even though I married outside my race, even now, I still feel very Chinese in my thinking. But that's the way it goes. It's strange now when I look back, so many of the ones who were so mean to me back then have children who married outside. I don't know if that had anything to do with it, but these people are all nice and friendly to me now. So it wasn't until literally just a few years ago that I started getting back with the community. I guess time, time sort of eased everything....

As time went by, my parents' attitude towards the marriage also changed. And then, Mo was really good to them. They could also see how well he was treating me. I guess at first, they thought we were going to move to the West Indies and they'd never see me again. I think that's what hurt my mom the most. But when she could see that we were going to settle in Halifax, then well, we sort of patched things up.

My husband and I both feel that no matter what race you are, as my brother puts it, whether you're polka-dot green or whatever, it's the person that counts — it's not the colour.

SHIRLEY WELSH

Before I got married, I was scared of marriage — especially a mixed marriage. In the small town I'm from, the majority of the girls were pregnant — only four girls in my class *didn't* get pregnant.

The pregnant ones quit school at grade ten or eleven, so by grade twelve there were hardly any girls left (laugh). Our principal said once you're pregnant, you can't come back to school.

When I married Jim — married out — I was disowned. I feel I can talk about it *now*, but for years it bothered me when I talked about it. Everything has been ironed out now. When I was growing up, I almost forgot that I was Chinese. It never occurred to me that my parents would disapprove. When I brought him home, that's when it really hit home base, and I thought, "Oh, hold it — it's not going to work." They said that if I married out of the Chinese race, then I would be disowned completely. But I felt that if I married someone whom I didn't love, eventually we'd get a divorce — then for sure they'd point the finger at me, that it's all my fault and everything. I thought I should base my decision on how *I* feel, and marry someone I really love. And to this day, I don't regret it.

FERN HUM

One significant thing in Sudbury, when I was about seventeen or eighteen, I started going out with guys against my parents' wishes.

I was being a very rebellious person, going out with non-Chinese guys. When I was in my last year of high school and first year of college, I went out with this French Canadian fellow. It was just somebody to go places with — movies, ice-skating, dances. It wasn't anything serious. I guess I wanted to be so much like a Canadian person, a non-Chinese person. Maybe I didn't want to admit to myself what I really was. So I would continue to go out with these non-Chinese fellows and do things that all the other young Canadians were doing. I would just say to my parents, "I don't want to listen to you! I know what I'm doing!"

When I was in my third year of college I met my husband, Doug. We got married a short time later. I got married when I was twenty-one, straight out of college. There's really not much I can compare with. When you're married with no children, there's still a fair amount of freedom involved. You're not tied to a schedule...

Doug is Canadian-born Chinese. So we sort of have similar frustrations. But his Chinese is a lot better than mine is and he's the only child in the family, so his parents depended on him a lot for translation. My mother is amazed that he helps me with household chores and the children. Doug would feed them, bathe them, change their diapers — and my mother would say, "You're dad never did *that!* It's a good thing you're getting Doug to do that."

My mother never used — I don't think she used anything, except for trying to get her tubes tied, but it didn't work (laugh). Actually, when we got to the age when we were talking about things like contraception, she was past menopause. Then I asked her, "Why didn't you ever get Dad to use the condom?" She said he would never use it. "Your father didn't want to use *anything*." She also said that the doctors never talked to her about birth control, whereas my gynecologist asked me about it after I had my first baby. See, my gynecologist is Caucasian. I guess when they're not of the same race, maybe you don't feel as embarrassed (laugh) to talk about it....

VALERIE MAH

My first exposure to other Chinese came in 1956 or 1957 at a Presbyterian Church congress in Toronto. It was very thrilling for me, as a young person living in a small town, to go to the city and meet other Chinese from across Canada. I mean that's enough to throw your head. I had never before had a Chinese boyfriend or even really met any Chinese guys. I met a young Chinese university student in Toronto who had gone with many girls. I was so flattered because he went back to Vancouver and broke off with his girlfriend and started writing to me.

Also in the 1950s, I went up to what was called the "Chinese matrimonial camp" in Geneva Park in Lake Couchiching. This was an attempt to bring together Chinese Americans and Chinese Canadians. I think it was started by the Chinese Canadian Association. It would attract at least 100 to 150 Chinese Canadians and Americans. They would spend a week up there in the summertime.

My oldest sister married Chinese. My brother married a Canadian girl from the Maritimes. My youngest sister married an Italian Jew. We used to say that, at least if you married Japanese, the children would look the same — that was important. But once one sister had married a non-Chinese, you kind of got over the hump. I guess because my mother was more broad-minded, there wouldn't have been the objection. There probably would have been more objection if my father had been alive.

My husband, Daniel, is Chinese. When I started going with him, he said it was fifty per cent easier going out with a Chinese girl because his mother could say to me, "How much money are you making?" and I wouldn't say, "It's none of your business," because I know that that's a typical question. Or if you're eating a meal, and you say, "How much did this food cost?" English people would say, "How insulting!" But the Chinese consider this a typical question and don't get upset.

When Daniel met me he said he knew that I wanted to marry his friend. But if I talked to this other guy about my work, he'd say, "I have enough troubles in my life. Don't talk to me about your troubles." But Daniel is so quiet and he's such a good listener. He's always encouraged me to do my own thing. He's never pushed me, and he's never held me back.

I knew Daniel was serious when he asked me out for breakfast because he's very much a night person. I chose him because we got along so well. Finally, I told the other guy that I didn't want to see him anymore. He asked how I could choose Daniel over him. You see, he was an engineer — he had money. First, you think somebody's going to earn all this money and take care of you. But then you find that getting along well with a person and having someone you like being with is more important — somebody whose shoulder you can cry on.

So instead of being typical, marrying a Chinese guy and staying at home, looking after the kids — with him being the bread-winner, I married Daniel. We had a son and I was off for a year, and then he said, "Such a talent would be wasted if you stay home." So off I went back to work again. I've been working ever since. He's always patiently waited while I did my thing. I mean who's going to put up with a wife who goes off to night school and works full-time? When I went to night courses he was never mad. When I went to work, he watched our son until we found daycare. He freelances, does advertising. He's his own boss. He never says that I have to stay at home, or that I should be home at nine. There was none of that. He just let me go.

LIL LEE

Well, I didn't get married until I was twenty-seven years old. It was unusual because most of my friends were already married by then and had families. No, I didn't date. I lived in a small town and there weren't too many boys my age. And a lot of them, you knew them so well, you know, they were almost like brothers to you. So there wasn't any ... (laugh) ... attraction.

My married aunts would come back to Nanaimo every now and then to visit the old homestead. One year, one of my aunts came from New York with her younger son. In those days a lot of girls didn't travel at all, but my youngest sister and I travelled with my aunt all through the United States to New York. And then we travelled alone back to Canada. I think my aunt actually planned to get my sister and me married off. But her plan didn't work (laugh). We just went for the free trip (laugh). She introduced us to a lot of people. Well you know, we'd meet these fellows. They'd take us out, and we'd size each other up. I don't know what was wrong with us. We were very particular, I suppose. Nothing turned up. I think it's because we didn't live in Chinatown — our thinking was a little bit different. We were not quite as old-fashioned and stifled. We mixed with a lot of Canadians. That probably affected our thinking too....

My husband, Wally, is originally from China. He came to Vancouver to attend the University of British Columbia. At first, I hesitated to go out with him. He was from China, and you had to think about China boys, you know (laugh). Their background is very different from ours. There's a language barrier to begin with. Some of them don't speak English that fluently. We, being Canadian-born, were comfortable speaking English. And although we can speak Chinese, it's a different dialect. So when you go out, you just can't converse freely with them. But with Wally, his English was pretty good. He came over in '49. He'd already graduated from Sun Yatsen University. He was quite modern in many ways. He liked dancing and partying — something I was never encouraged to do, coming from a small town. I wasn't too agile on my feet when it came to dancing. He said, "You're just like a stone" (laugh). He already knew how to do all the dance steps, and he was very popular with the ladies. Oh yes, quick waltz, slow waltz, tango, foxtrot — you name it — all the ballroom dances he knew (laugh). Oh, dating is probably the best time of your life, right?

I could have married somebody very rich too (laugh), you know, in those days with all this matchmaking. Well, a lot of my friends did marry people who were well-to-do. I guess they're fairly happy — if that's their priority. I don't know, money wasn't really all that important to me. I felt that it's better to marry somebody you respect and like — not somebody whose money you respect, but whom you don't really like (laugh). My sister felt quite differently. She married somebody who was quite well-to-do. A lot of my friends, you know, just listened to their parents, got married and raised their families. My parents — they were just average, old-fashioned types who never encouraged the girls to be independent. But I suppose the years running the family store probably made me more independent.

LINDA LEE

I got married the summer after the first year of law school — June, 1974. I met Bill in high school, but we didn't really go out until our college years. Before Bill, I dated some Chinese boys, mainly foreign students. There was a Chinese University Students' Group that I belonged to at university. It seemed that I didn't have a whole lot in common with the "overseas Chinese boys." I think it's the difference in cultural backgrounds. Conflict wouldn't be the right word. It's more like going on tracks that don't quite come together. While we had being Chinese in common, there were other things which were different, whether it was the movies we had seen, or the music that we were listening to. I remember once on a double date, a blind date for me, the movie was slightly risque. My Chinese date found it terribly embarrassing to sit there and watch this romantic movie with a woman. And of course, I got embarrassed because he was embarrassed — and the whole thing was a complete disaster.

Whenever a Chinese boy came to pick me up, my parents were just *thrilled* (laugh) that I would have a Chinese date. And it got to be a much bigger thing than perhaps it should have been. So if an overseas Chinese boy came to take me out, it was hard for us to get out the door because my mother would want to question him about what he was studying, where he was from, his parents' background, and so on ... which made it hard for both of us. Like the typical teenager, I was embarrassed. "Good heavens, Mom!" My parents generally discouraged dates with Canadian boys. It was important to them that we marry Chinese.

My father died in 1968 before Bill and I were going seriously at all. But my father was alive when my sister was dating her Canadian husband, Peter ... and he made it quite difficult for them at times. For example, sometimes when Peter came to pick her up, my father would simply shut the door in his face (laugh). But when he was very ill, he gave them his blessing.

By the time Bill and I had decided to marry, my mother already had a very good Canadian son-in-law. Although, I think if she had had a completely free choice, she would have liked to have had at least one son-in-law who spoke Chinese. But she managed to communicate with Bill and Peter just fine.

When my sisters and I were teenagers and we were watching some romantic movie on TV, with couples riding off into the sunset, I remember a few times my father said to us, "Don't believe any of that." He would tell us that love is a nonsensical basis for a marriage and that we should be careful not to marry for love. I think he was worried that my sister and I would marry non-Chinese Canadians without having thought it out. I think he was afraid we'd get hurt. And perhaps — and I'm guessing, he believed that Chinese men took more responsibility with their women folk. I don't really know.

LILY WELSH

I met my husband in Edmonton in 1972 when I was working at a restaurant part-time. My husband used to live upstairs. He used to come down with his friends all the time. Actually, his friend matched us up. It was kind of funny, really. One night he asked me to go out and I didn't really want to because I was kind of leery about going out with people I did not know. But when I found out that he had a Chinese sister-in-law, I got quite interested. After that I continued to go out with him and found that he was quite nice.

Tom is a fairly easygoing person. He tries to understand and respect my customs. So he's really no problem. My dad and mom weren't really that concerned, until we started getting quite serious. My father wanted to let me know that the decision was my decision, but he wanted me to be sure that it was what I really wanted. Actually, when Tom and I were getting pretty close, I started getting kind of worried.... I wondered what other people would say. Then I didn't want to go out with him anymore. It just seemed like we were breaking off, and then we got back together again. So I had conflict in me, really. I felt like I didn't want to go out with him — I wanted to find a Chinese guy. Yet before Tom, I did go out with a few Chinese guys, but umm ... nothing ever materialized. I still liked being with Tom, even though inside me I felt like, "Gee, if I could just meet and really get serious with a Chinese guy...." But after some time I just wasn't finding the right

Chinese person, so I gave up looking. Then I changed my attitude and said to myself, "Oh, maybe I'll see how it works with Tom." We went together quite a few years before we got married.

Tom was very well accepted in the family. My parents were quite open-minded about the marriage. But then Tom is a really good person. He's helped my family a lot — and my family really appreciated the help he's given them. My father speaks English very well. I think he feels more relaxed being with Tom than he does with his Chinese sons-in-law....

ROSE LUMB

I wasn't too interested in dating until I was into my teens and we usually had a lot of Oriental boys who would ask us to school dances. I was never really asked out by any Caucasian guys.... I started going steady with my husband when I was sixteen (laugh). So I went with him for seven years, and we've been married for thirty-five years. I just happened to have been lucky to have met the right one and had no opportunities like the young ones nowadays to kind of (laugh) flip around as they say. Oh ... there would have been other opportunities, I suppose, through the bank, or different dances, but I never gave it to much thought. As soon as I met him at the Chinese public school, I decided that we would go out together and it developed into a nice friendship. And I was never interested in somebody else after that.

CAROLINE CHAN

My mom kept me very sheltered. I wasn't allowed to date. She never liked any of the boys I brought home. My grandmother used to freak out when I brought any boys home. I remember she physically threw out one of my friends. He wasn't a boyfriend. He was just a friend who happens to be a male. It's so funny because John and I are still really good friends now. We were working on a science project at my house. My grandmother *freaked out!* She started screaming, "How could you bring a boy into the house?" It was broad daylight. We were just doing school work together. John didn't know what my grandmother was screaming about —

she was yelling at him in Chinese ... You see, John's Caucasian. My family has no qualms at all about Chinese boys. It seems to be a preoccupying fear that we're going to marry Caucasians. It bothers them, I guess. It doesn't bother me. It's a fact of life. We live in a white society — what can you do?

First of all, if I marry, I'd like to marry somebody who is Chinese — okay? It's important that my husband — should I ever find one, feel as strongly about being Chinese as I do — because it's important to me.

OUR CHILDREN,
A NEW GENERATION

ROSE LUMB

I think that I was firm with my children, but because I was brought up here in Canada, I believe in some ways I was a little bit more lax, more umm … understanding with the children, because I knew that they were really in a new generation from what we were brought up in. You know, our parents came from the old country. And I believe that we were fortunate to be in the middle. We could see where there were things that we wouldn't do — things our parents expected us to do. I would never send my children out berry-picking when they were young. My mother mostly wanted us to be involved with our Chinese church and to help out the Chinese community whenever asked — like when I was asked to sit on the Chinese Consolidated Benevolent Association float in the Victoria Day parade.

I've always instilled in the children that they should have respect for their elders. And my children were very fortunate that my father came to live with us for nine years. We always thought that was one of our greatest joys — that the children were fortunate enough to have had their grandfather living with them for nine years. It was my father who imparted a lot of Chinese stories to the children. And they loved and respected him.

Well, being a mother was the hardest role I believe, because in those days there was no TV, no second car like young mothers have these days, and no nannies. We had to do all our own work and take care of our children, making sure they went to their classes and did well in school. When the children were young, you didn't get much sleep at night. It was such a busy life. Taking care of four children was a lot of work! I had those four children within the space of seven years, you see…. Oh, I managed somehow. This is why I decided that it was best to stay home with the children for the first eleven years.

I'm happy that women have come out of the shell. They have privileges to do much more than in my early days. The opportunity there for young people, especially women, is phenomenal.

FERN HUM

Neither of my parents beat or spanked us. I feel that there's a way of disciplining a child up until a certain age, an age when they can understand the difference between right and wrong. My parents believed in that too, that you teach them first and then, if they are misbehaving, you do something to change their misbehaviour. I think I was spanked only once, and that was for something *really* wrong... There's no margin for error. They can't sort of think, "Well, maybe it's wrong and maybe it's right." Let's say Jessica goes out on the street and she knows she's not supposed to cross the street by herself, yet she does it anyway. Then I would spank her to make sure she understands it. But I think I would restrain from corporal punishment until I know for sure they understand.

I think in terms of role models, I'd like both kids to see Doug and myself performing equal kinds of activities, not just Mommy washing dishes and cleaning house — and not just Daddy using a hammer and doing all the repairs in the house. I think I'd like to see my children trying to take on all kinds of activities and be comfortable doing them. Jessica has seen me hammering. I took a course in woodworking (laugh) a couple of years ago. I made a little table.

For my children, I'm hoping that they would grow up with some knowledge of the Chinese culture, although I know it's going to be difficult for them since both Doug and myself don't speak Chinese at home. Our first language is English. Yes, our children are going to the Heritage Language classes at public school.

For myself, I think my husband and I are looking forward to retirement. Well, we were talking about it the other day and I said to him, "I'd like to retire in Vancouver." There's no ice and no snow there. (laugh)

CAROLINE CHAN

I really want my children, *at least,* to be able to speak Chinese. It's important for them to realize that. Just for them to say that we belong isn't enough. They have to feel that ... we are people — we are Canadians ... and that Canada is a mixture of people of all nationalities. We are one people. We should be able to relate to one another. Some day my children are going to be Canadian through and through, but they have Chinese heritage. And I hope that they would never feel the prejudice I felt — just because of my skin colour and just because of their heritage. In a few generations, they're going to be so Canadianized they might not even know what Chinese is. I feel the need to belong, and I feel a need that they should feel that I should belong, you know.... I don't know how to say it. Deep inside I want them to feel that Chinese people here are Canadian, just like they are — it's important.

BETTY TOY

I think the Chinese Canadian woman can make a contribution to society by helping younger women in the community coming up in the ranks, making it easier for them. I mean, somebody who's already established in a career could give younger women a break by hiring them, giving emotional support. Just giving of herself to make it easier for the next generation.

Right now I'm not thinking long term. But one day I'd like to get married. I'd like to have maybe one or two kids. My Chinese heritage is important to me, so I would want it to be important to my children. Everybody likes to know where they come from — and likes to hear stories about their grandmothers or whatever. I wouldn't overdo ... because we have to live in this society and this is not China. Chinese heritage to me is history — it's culture, the language, the food — the people. I can't say that I know a lot about it, but it's everything that has come and gone before you.

MAY CHEUNG

At first I didn't know about family planning. I was very stupid then. I wouldn't have had five children if I'd known. Two children is more than enough. I didn't know about any contraceptive methods until I already had five children (laugh). I don't know why I hadn't dared to ask about it before.

Sometimes my children help me with housework. I have two sons and three daughters. My eldest daughter helps me the most. I don't differentiate sons from daughters — I treat them equally. I ask my sons to do housework, but they don't do it. My youngest daughter always complains about that, but there is nothing I can do.

I hope my children will be able to get a good education and good jobs. My eldest daughter is now a pharmacist. My children are very active. They can mix with the *gui* very well. I certainly would not be pleased if my children married "foreigners." It's definitely better for us Chinese to marry Chinese. Those *gui* don't know anything (laugh). That's that. But that's only what I hope. Sure, I talk with my children about it, why not? But it's up to them to decide.

LINDA LEE

When Andrew was little, not only did my mother spend a lot of time with him, but at night when she slept in his room, I would hear her talking to him. She'd be teaching Andrew to count, or she'd be teaching him parts of the body, or Chinese phrases. If someone said this, then you say that, or if someone asks you how old you are, this is how you say how old you are. So all that stuff Andrew remembers.

And the other thing that he remembers is Chinese food, because when my mother was alive, she would cook Chinese since she didn't know how to cook anything else. So now we go out to Chinese restaurants quite a bit because Andrew loves Chinese food. So he has those things left. This past Chinese New Year's he took some Chinese things, like the red money envelope, to school for "Show and Tell".... He's already aware. He knows that he's half Chinese. In fact, for a time there, we had trouble trying to teach him that he was half Chinese. He wanted to say that he was *all* Chinese. He couldn't understand the *half* parts.... Without my mother here, I think it will be harder for my daughter, Julia, to understand any Chinese, and maybe some of the other things that my mother would do for the Chinese festivals.

I haven't thought seriously about sending my children to Chinese school. Actually, we're thinking about French immersion. So much of what my children see is non-Chinese — while when I was growing up, a lot of people around me were Chinese. We all spoke Chinese. With my mother's passing, there's no one that I talk to in Chinese on a regular basis with my children present. So their likelihood of learning Chinese is going to be slim. But we do attend the Chinese society functions. Of course, we still have a lot of Mom's old friends whom we see from time to time.

TAM GOOSEN

So far I've had great communication with my children. We talk a lot. We read the newspaper together every morning and discuss politics. My older daughter decided to do a project on Chinese Canadian women, so I was able to help her. Sharing the same language is a big asset. We mainly speak in English, and my kids have also been able to learn Cantonese. My mother lives in the neighbourhood and comes over almost every day to make dinner for them. They love her and try to use whatever Cantonese they have. This helps them through the Heritage Language classes. My children also know Japanese because we lived in Japan for a year.

As far as our situation is concerned, I don't feel there is any cultural identity problem for our children. First of all, Toronto is a very mixed city ethnically, which is very good. We live in a Portuguese and Chinese neighbourhood. Many of our friends are mixed couples too. And because Ted, my husband, is involved in East Asian Studies, we have a lot of Japanese and Chinese friends. My kids generally perceive themselves as Chinese Canadians, but they are also very much aware of the fact that their father is not Chinese. Schoolmates often ask them, "Are you English or Chinese?" But I always tell them, "Your father's from the States. You mother's Chinese — and you were born in Canada." So sometimes we try to increase their awareness of their cultural heritages and encourage them to see the mixture as a positive experience — the best of both worlds.

Raising children is a very personal business. I don't feel that our different cultural backgrounds have caused any problems in raising our children. In general, our ways are different from those of my mother's generation. But of course, if I had married a Chinese and lived with a Chinese mother-in-law, the Chinese influence in raising kids would be much greater. But now I am more influenced by what a modern mother in Canada should do. Basically, both parents have to have the same ideas about parenting, otherwise problems arise.

I think it's very important for children to grow up in an environment where they can develop optimism, self-confidence and skills. If we fail to do that in our schools — where everything starts — the future can be pretty bleak. Canada is really a kind of social experiment, bringing together people from so many different cultures. It's easy to say that we have to work together, but the specific mechanics of working together are very important. Despite all the criticism, I think we have a very healthy public education system. We have to maintain it or we don't really have a future....

LIL LEE

My parents' marriage was just a traditional Chinese type of marriage: bring up the children quite strictly, don't encourage them to be on their own. But my generation, with my marriage, I've encouraged my four kids to be independent and go for higher education. Different sort of value systems. You have to compete now too, with fellow Canadians. In those days, even though you wanted to, you didn't have the opportunity. Being a mother, you're always the teacher in a way (laugh). Although they're grown-up, they're still your children. My mother, she's eighty-nine, and she still worries about me (laugh).

My children have been exposed to a lot of Chinese culture. If I had married a Canadian or Chinese Canadian, I think the upbringing of my children would be entirely different. But with my husband, a lot of his values are still Chinese. A lot of Chinese

Canadians say, "Oh, I'm not interested in China, or anything Chinese." But my kids are different. They're very interested in China and Chinese. In fact, they all want to go back to study in China, to learn the language. We did take our whole family back to China one year when my youngest daughter was about thirteen. We took them to my husband's village, and showed them the house he lived in, where he got his water. They found it really fascinating, you know, tracing your roots. In fact, a lot of my friends are quite surprised my children are so interested in China and interested in helping the Chinese community. They want their own children to be like that. I guess we encouraged them when they were young, telling them that, although they're born in Canada, their heritage is Chinese, their father's motherland is China.

COMING OF AGE

VICTORIA YIP

In a woman's life there's a time for everything — a time for school, a time for marriage, a time for motherhood, a time for yourself and a time to retire. I didn't retire until the age of sixty-nine. Now all my friends and relatives say they can never get me at home. Either I'm out shopping or visiting relatives. I want to have my exercise, but there's no fun just doing exercise. So I go to the stores and see a lot of new things. I also garden. I like to take the bus and go see what other parts of the city are like. I'm so busy, even though there's nothing to show for it.

I'd say that my life is quite interesting now. All my sisters-in-law just stay home day after day — don't go anywhere or do anything. I like to travel, but a lot of Chinese, including some of my relatives, never go beyond Pender Street, never mind about going to another city. I say, "Why are you afraid of going?" If I want to go to Nanaimo, I just hop on a bus and go. If I don't know where to go, I just ask the people on the street. Ask — you know English, you can't get lost. Self-confidence is very important. But because these Chinese never go out, they don't develop self-confidence.

I live for today. I'm a person who doesn't dwell on the past. I know lots of old people who do nothing else but talk about the past. I'm really forgetful about my past....

When you grow older, you have more peace of mind. I think peace of mind is very important to old people. As you grow older you have more faith that everything's going to work out okay. No matter how hard or difficult life becomes, it turns out okay in the end. I think faith is the most important thing. You have to have faith in life, faith in God. I think that young people should have that kind of faith, especially with the nuclear threat. I find young people today much more aware.

During the late 1960s and 1970s, there were a lot of hippies, free spirits and all that. Before I met any of them, I used to say,

"Oh … it'd be terrible to be a hippie! Why on earth do they want to be hippies?" Then when I worked at Ming-Wah, lots of hippies used to come in to buy the cast-iron pots for cooking out on farms or camping in the mountains. I asked them, "Why do you want to live that way?" They explained it to me. Now I really, really respect them, because they are willing to forgo material things. Okay, just a small example — they'd come in and say, "Don't waste your paper or plastic bags, we'll put our purchases in this basket." I really respect them for what they think. They are really quite courageous — doing things completely different from their parents.

I don't feel the aging. I mean, your eyes get dimmer, so you have to wear glasses. Your teeth have to be replaced and you have to get a hearing aid. Growing old does bother you, but then after a while you accept it. That's part of growing old. I'm very fortunate to be in fairly good health, and I can still walk fast. When we went to China for a visit, my son kept saying, "Slow down! We can't keep up with you." I celebrated my 65th birthday in Shanghai…. That was my first visit to China. I never thought that I'd be able to go see Beijing, as I had always dreamed….

GRACE LEE

The families now are different from before. In the olden days, the family always had to stay together. This was not necessarily good because in families like ours, the father had to be solely responsible for the whole family. Old people would get upset if their children didn't look after them.

The young now don't want us old people's money. They can earn their own money. Even though you could say it was old-fashioned, at least there was a concept of family in the old days. Now the children of wealthier families all go their own ways when they grow older. This is no good. Whatever they earn now, they spend. They won't save any money.

When I had my eye operation, my mother came to visit from China three times by herself. She always wanted me to go back to China, but I gave her money for airfare and she came four times by plane. I was so frugal that in seven years I didn't even buy one new piece of clothing. My mother didn't know. She thought I made a lot of money.

On the last trip, she didn't return to China because she fell down in the kitchen after she was here for only three days. I hated retiring at that time even though I was in my sixties.

I had bought an old home, renovated it myself and moved in. But when I turned eighty, I told myself that I shouldn't be so stubborn. What would I do if I got sick? I was prepared to move to a more suitable place when this place was built. My former pupils cared about me and were always concerned that I be well looked after. When I made up my mind to come to this nursing home, they were all delighted. Everybody here is so nice. The administrator, the nurse's aides, the cooks — all the staff here are so good to me. No wonder I feel so contented.

I have also joined the association for the blind. Every week they send around a car to pick me up to go to the meeting of the White Cane Club, an organization for helping blind people. After the meeting we have entertainment such as music. When I was eighty, I joined the swimming club. Everyone was amazed that an eighty year-old woman would be willing to learn how to swim. The exercise is excellent for my health. I tell other old people that they must exercise or they will get aches and pains all over.

ANNE FONG

I want security now. I wish I had higher aspirations. But I think to be a woman and older is a difficult thing, especially in this culture where all the stress is on youth. You know, you read about women over a certain age, poverty-stricken. It's not true that they marry and live happily ever after. They are dependent on the men for financial security. I think every woman, from the time she is young, should develop her own career and financial security, for her person alone, for her own self-esteem.

SPEAKING FOR OURSELVES

TAM GOOSEN

I got involved in the NDP when somebody literally knocked on my door and asked me to join the party. I had read about the NDP and I had always been interested in politics when I was in school, so I thought it was time to see politics in action. I wanted to know what real democracy was and how to achieve it, not just from the knowledge of books. When I came here, I had to bury myself in books. I wouldn't have known how the actual participation works if I hadn't tried it myself. As far as the local participation of citizens is concerned, the democratic system of residents' associations is probably the most effective forum for getting the attention of politicians. For instance, people who just arrive from Hong Kong could be very ignorant about the politics here. When they really want to have some kind of voice in the community, not just Chinatown, they can go through the parent associations at their kids' school — or they can turn to their local Member of Parliament or City Hall about their grievances. Still, the forum where they can make the most noise and do some arm wrestling is probably the residents' associations.

My actual participation in politics began during Winnie Ng's first nomination fight against Dale Martin. I found out that I was one of the few Chinese on the NDP list. So of course, they rounded me up. Then with Olivia Chow's campaign for school trustee, I got a fuller view of what a political campaign in Canada was all about. I got to find out more about the work of the school trustee. Then as my own two children were growing up, I started examining parents' rights and the role of parents' associations in exercising those rights. So it was the combination of those two things — my interest in politics and my interest in my own kids' education — that made it easier to say "yes" when the opportunity came along. I never thought I was really going to jump into it, but one of the trustees in Ward Eight was retiring and there were a lot of boundary changes in the riding. I ended up running against a very powerful incumbent, Nola Crewes. Nobody thought I could win against her, but I managed to do it.

I did encounter racism during both my campaigns. People would be fairly polite about it because I was running with an Anglo partner. But when we went door-to-door together, people would often just look at my partner, directing their questions at her and ignoring me as though I was just an ethnic sidekick. Subtle signs like that. Some people were shocked that a Chinese would be running. One time on Queen Street a kid actually spat on me. But when you're in politics, you have to develop a tough skin. I couldn't let it depress me. You have to look at the positive and convince yourself that you have to go through all this to prove to people you can do it. It's a tough business. You have to knock at every door — and you have no idea what you're going to find behind each door. Sometimes it can be exhilarating. I've had wonderful conversations with people about politics and education — but other times it's pretty scary.

I don't know what lies ahead for me in the future in terms of my political career. Electoral politics is something that depends on what kinds of opportunities are there and whether or not you're ready to seize them. It's timing — and luck as well. I think people go into politics for different reasons. Some people are very ambitious and know exactly where they want to be at a certain point in time. I'm kind of reluctant to set such goals. As an active participant, I am still very curious about the whole process. I've always been an observer, observing my colleagues — their interactions with each other and with bureaucrats. I watch all levels of government. That's what keeps me alert, so I don't really concern myself with future ambitions.

I'm into my second term as a school trustee in Toronto. I've realized that the education system touches a lot of lives. It's a lot more accessible to the community than any other level of government. Concerns about whether or not a child is reading. Concerns about the environment or racism. Misunderstandings between parents and teachers. A school trustee is really a very hands-on kind of politician. There's not a huge gap between you and the parents — or the students and the teachers. I've met a lot of fairly progressive educators. Overall, it has been a very positive, encouraging experience.

The great thing about being a school trustee is the opportunity I've had to work with many different people. I'm involved with the Race Relations committee, the Native Students' committee and the Heritage Language committee. It's a great experience to have. I've learned that if you want to get something done, you have to get involved. The work that's been done in anti-racist education is encouraging, but there's still a lot more that needs to be done. We still don't have enough material for each and every teacher in the system. One of my immediate goals is to make sure that all teachers feel comfortable and knowledgeable enough to introduce anti-racist education in the classroom.

What worries me now is the fact that I am the only visible minority on the school board. Electoral politics can be very hard on visible minorities because it becomes like a popularity contest. We have a real disadvantage that way. It is very important to encourage visible minorities to form a collective to make sure that their rights are being protected — otherwise we'll be totally silenced. It doesn't matter how progressive the majority group is. You can be progressive and yet blind, not intentionally. Most of the time they don't even realize it. It's so important to hear different voices — literally different voices, different ethnic groups, different socio-economic groups. It's just too easy for the more articulate group to have a total monopoly. The process is very slow, but it has to happen.

I think it's very important for people to speak for themselves. I do not view myself as a spokesperson for the Chinese Canadian community. It's very tempting for people outside of a community to generalize and only want to talk to a small segment of a community — because they don't want to deal with the complexity of that community. And it's easy for people inside a community to grasp the chance to speak for the entire community, but I think it's important to avoid this because it's open to manipulation from all directions. Every single person should be given the opportunity and tools to speak for themselves.

VALERIE MAH

I do a lot of MCing in the community, mainly for Mon Sheong, a home for Chinese seniors.[1] I just size up the audience. I've never had any formal training in public speaking. I feel embarrassed at times because I don't know enough Chinese. My memory is such that I'm very poor at languages, but I usually understand.

I'm the kind of person who has so many things going on that I wish I had ten, twenty more hours in a day. My son gets angry and says I'm a workaholic. He says that even if there wasn't any work, I'd find it. I'm like my mother. I thrive on work. I like to organize things. For example, I like being treasurer at Mon Sheong.

I feel very honoured to be on the Advisory Council on Multi-culturalism. But I don't really know all the problems in the community. I don't believe you can handle everything. But I think I should be doing a lot more than I am, even now. I wish I had more time to become more involved in the community. I wish I knew a little more Chinese, so I could do more things. I'd still like to see a Chinese cultural centre.

When it comes down to it all, I have a little more high profile than a lot of women. I've been on CBC and CTV. It was lovely and I was thrilled to be on TV. Yet, at first, it bothered me because I was afraid people would say, "How come she's on when she doesn't speak Chinese?" Then I felt, "Well, damn it all. You work hard for the community, so don't let the nasty comments bother you." It doesn't even bother me when people call me *juk sing*. I always took it as a joke since I didn't understand how derogative it was meant to be.

My second sister, Ruth, has also been an outspoken member of the Chinese community. She's a real libber…. She was involved in a very famous human rights case in Dresden, Ontario. She was with some blacks, and they were refused service at a restaurant. She made a big case about it. Her picture was even in the papers. That was a trial case for human rights. That's the kind of person she is. If ever there was somebody with lots of nerve, that would be my sister, Ruth!

ROSE LUMB

In the 1960s my husband became interested in politics. He was still working for his father when he became an alderman. He just seemed to get into politics by accident really. He was asked to run and he thought, "Well, here's an opportunity for a Chinese Canadian to get into something for his municipality." And when he did run, he topped the polls. So it was quite a feat for him. Ed was very well-liked and always generous with his time for any worthy cause.

When I wasn't running our motel business or helping Ed with his municipal work, I was doing volunteer work in the Chinese community. In June, 1986, I was very privileged to receive the Honourary Citizen of Victoria award for my forty years of volunteer service.

My work began at the veterans' hospital in the Red Cross lodge, serving coffee to the veterans. I have also had the opportunity of working in the Canadian Immigration Welcoming Committee, welcoming the new Chinese immigrants. And I've helped the Chinatown Lions through their projects, as well as the Chinatown Care Centre. I've been involved in many other interesting projects, but it's hard for me to list them all down. It just seems that the main thing is being involved in the community in whatever way I can — whether I'm asked to be a guest speaker at a banquet or go out to schools to speak to children about Chinese New Year.

I feel that whenever I'm out there in front of the public, I've always felt that I'm not just representing myself. I'm here on behalf of all Chinese Canadian women. I've always sort of thought of them in my mind all the time. I'm here because I have the *privilege* of representing the rest of the Chinese ladies in our community, you know.

IRENE CHU

In 1979 I took the job of coordinator for a provincial conference, "Living and Growing in Canada: a Chinese Canadian Perspective." Over five hundred people participated. The conference served as a kick-off point for the anti-$W5^2$ campaign which spread like a wild prairie fire across seventeen major cities in the country. The anti-$W5$ movement culminated in the formation of the Chinese Canadian National Council (for Equality) in April 1980, after CTV issued an apology for their racially discriminating attitudes.

In late 1979 or early 1980, President Ham of the University of Toronto called a meeting of about thirty high-profiled members of the Chinese community. He wanted to establish two fellowship grants to be awarded to students of Chinese Canadian Studies. The amount was $13,000 in total. But the University was only going to fund the first year, and Dr. Ham requested the community to pick up the responsibility from the second year on. All those at the meeting cheered the proposal and accepted the challenge. Come the second year, no one wanted to have anything to do with the project. It was embarrassing — something had to be done. I gathered together a few women and we jointly organized a fashion show featuring Chinese Canadian designers. We raised $30,000 for the University.

That event served as a springboard for my subsequent involvements in various non-Chinese charitable organizations — the Canadian Cancer Society Fashion, the Canadian Breast Cancer Foundation, Urban Alliance on Race Relations....

On most of the boards or committees I was routinely looked upon as a double token — a woman and a member of a visible minority. Tokenism or not, I felt it was important that I would serve as a bridge or link between the Chinese community and the larger society. Whenever I was the only non-white participant I would try to facilitate the involvement of other non-white Canadians, such as people of Black, Korean and Filipino origin.

I recall that during the anti-$W5$ movement I always presented myself as a housewife because I was proud to be a mother and wife. On one occasion the then leader of the NDP, obviously impressed with my active role in the anti-$W5$ campaign, approached to talk to me. He asked what was my profession. When I said I was a housewife, his face dropped three inches. He immediately turned around and abandoned me.

Such was the general attitude towards what I termed as one of the most disadvantaged groups of women — housewives and single mothers, as well as farm women. They are looked down upon as second class citizens by society in general simply because their work is not measured in dollars and cents. Yet they perform some of the most taxing, demanding and important tasks for our country. I fought for pension for homemakers and lobbied for more back-up services and programs to draw women out of their houses.

RAMONA MAR

When the W5 controversy was just heating up, I went to a Chinese Benevolent Association (C.B.A.) meeting to find out what it was all about and sat there quietly taking notes until they showed the actual part of the program that was being contested. Well, I was furious! So when they passed around a list of people willing to help protest this program, I signed up, not as a journalist, but as a member of Vancouver's Chinese Canadian community. Then all of a sudden, I found myself a member of the C.B.A. Adhoc Committee Against W5.... Well, I handed out leaflets on street corners. I marched and got petitions signed, and on and on....

By the time I got involved in the Pender Guy radio collective, I was also working part-time at Sears, going to the B.C. Institute of Technology, writing for Uncle Roy's newspaper — and working with the W5 committee.... All this was going on in my life when a few of my friends from the Taiwan trip decided to visit. We arranged a small reunion of sorts over Christmas at a disco. We were told it would cost $5 each just for the cover charge. We thought it was an outrageously high price, so we decided to go elsewhere. Later on, someone in the group said, "Oh, they always charge Orientals $5, didn't you know that?" I said, "You must be kidding! This is 1980! There are laws against that!" Naturally, I didn't believe it. Well, to test the rumour, I phoned the night club the next day and discovered, yes, it was regularly a $3 cover charge. When I told them we were asked for $5 the previous night, they said someone must have made a mistake. But other Chinese told me similar stories about this disco. Wow, was I angry! Eventually, we were directed to the B.C. Human Rights Branch.

As part of the investigation, we had to see if this discrimination would happen again. Sure enough it did. The *white* human rights officer walked up to the door and was charged $3 entry. Then we, a group of about eight Asian Canadians, followed behind. "Five dollars," we were told by — of all people — a Chinese Canadian man at the door! This was too much for me. I began to argue that we were told $3 over the phone. He disagreed, saying it was always $5. Then he looked at me and said, "I'm Chinese too, you know, why would I discriminate?" How could this man have said such a thing? His logic didn't hold water. Just because you have the same yellow skin, doesn't mean you don't discriminate! This incident still haunts me. It frightens me because it makes me realize that we can be our own worst enemies. Fellow Chinese Canadians hurting their own, hurting anyone. That's disgusting and sad at the same time.

Following the investigation, someone chose to teach me a lesson — and I always had my suspicions that it was directly related to my complaint to the Human Rights people. For a month afterwards, I got hate calls and hate mail. The person called about sixty times, calling at any time of day, sometimes hanging up, sometimes saying my name first. The letters were the worst part of the harassment. One of them even had a Chinese woman's face on it with the eyes slashed out. The paper was burnt all around it. It said, "You bitch." God, it was the most frightening time of my life. I was paranoid. I didn't want to go anywhere. I even walked around with a spray can of paint, in case my anonymous friend might confront me in some dark corner. The R.C.M.P. got nowhere with the case. The phone company never did trace the calls and it remains a mystery to this day. I will never, ever forget it. Was this the price one has to pay for speaking out against injustice? If it was, would I ever speak out again? Well, I guess the scare tactics made me all the more resolved to carry on, although I did consider dropping the case against the disco at one point. For a month, my mom and sisters and I lived in paranoia. But we didn't give up.

In the end, we won a $500 settlement from the Candy Store Discotheque, plus a public apology — big deal! We donated the money to the Chinese Cultural Centre, which was fundraising at that time for a new building. I suppose the donation was in part a recognition that the fight we had won was on behalf of all Chinese Canadians, even the guy at the door of the disco. We also did a documentary of this case for Pender Guy. That, along with a documentary on the *W5* case, won our radio station the B'nai B'rith Human Rights Media Award in the fall of 1980. It was quite a thrill because here we were, young Chinese Canadians — the targets of blatant discrimination by the media in the *W5* case, and by a private company in the disco case — documenting our own experience and getting recognition for that contribution!

The *W5* controversy and the disco incident showed me that we can make some change, and that it is crucial for us to speak out for ourselves. Nobody else will do it for us. Nobody else has this particular history or perspective. You begin to realize the importance of politics. Chinese Canadians should vote — vote for candidates who are most sensitive to their needs.

In July, 1983, when the Social Credit government brought in several pieces of controversial legislation, a new group was formed, Chinese Canadians for the Restoration of Human Rights. However, the group wasn't able to keep up the momentum. Unlike the *W5* issue, we weren't able to get the entire community mobilized over what we perceived to be an attack on our human rights. *W5*, on the other hand, was a targeted, specific fight. Here was the violation on video tape — you rally against it and get an apology.

FERN HUM

I started doing some volunteer work in the late 1970s at University Settlement House.[3] At that time there wasn't anyone else on the board who lived in the community, and we felt it was important to always have Chinese personnel since the area was seventy percent Chinese. So I got involved, serving on the community development and social services committee.

I felt very bitter and frustrated because of the difficulty of mobilizing the Chinese population to do anything. I found it difficult to get local Chinese people on committees — to spend

time looking at issues. Most of them were city planning issues....
It just strikes me that the Canadian-born Chinese here have a sort
of go-between role. In the Chinese tradition, they always say the
best thing is not to get involved with the government. These
Chinese will go to work, earn their own money, then stay at home.
Even though they were needled or pushed, like when there's
discrimination against them, they will not move. This attitude is
still ingrained in a lot of Chinese. But there have been some who
have been active.

I've been told that the reason we don't get very many Chinese
involved is that there's a small population — and it's mostly
people from overseas who are too busy working and taking care
of their families to do any other activities. But then, how can you
get so many out for, let's say, the *W5* issue? I think a lot of
promotion was done regarding this issue. You could actually *see*
the discrimination — and you know that the Chinese are very
anxious about their children's education. Many of them had the
W5 program translated into Chinese — yet they simply don't want
to get involved when it comes to smaller issues.

Another example is the heritage language issue which came
up in the schools. They were trying to get the Heritage Language
Program started in Scarborough schools, but not too many
Chinese Canadians came out to support it. We did get Heritage
Language Programs started in two public schools downtown.
There were enough parents in downtown Toronto who wanted to
start Chinese classes as part of the everyday curriculum.

MARY WONG

Because I did so much for the community — and for the Liberal
Party.... John Munro asked me to be a citizenship court judge. I
said, "Oh, yeah, yeah, yeah...." I didn't think I was really going
to get it. Well, I've never been the president of anything. I'm
always the vice-president in the Chinese community. I'm willing
to help, but I don't want to be the one in control of everything.
Like when I help, I want to make sure I do a good job.

I didn't build up my hopes on becoming a citizenship court
judge because my friend could change his mind about me. So

Thursday comes — and I know that's the day they make the appointment in the Privy Council. So Thursday night comes and still no phone call. And then on Friday, I get a call from John Munro's assistant, who says, "How are you, your Honour?" Well, I still didn't believe it. I had an appointment downtown, so I went. When I came back, the news was already on the air. The news media called to say that they'd be coming down to take my picture by five. "But I haven't got my hair done!" They told me to just be myself. They interviewed me over the phone and then came to take my picture. All my friends heard the news about me on the radio, so they came over. I was up until five in the morning. Everybody was so happy. The next day I flew to Ottawa. We got briefed for a few days. And on Tuesday, Trudeau read the changing of the citizenship act. About five hundred people were there. Trudeau turned to me and said, "Congratulations, Mary. You sure get around."

When the Status of Women came in, Judy LaMarsh asked me if I would like to go on the committee. Because of my lack of education, I didn't think I could do it. Then in terms of taking care of the restaurant, I didn't think I would like to travel across Canada.... But the job as judge was great. I really enjoyed it. I'm retired now. While I was a judge, I didn't bother with the restaurant — that would have been conflict of interest.

MAY MAH

When China suffered from famine around 1960, we helped out with the fundraising here. There weren't many activities here — not as many community agencies as there are today. When did I become really active? It's hard to say.... During the W5 controversy we ran around urging people to see films about the incident and so on. We also helped the Chinese Association and the school for overseas Chinese open a fundraising casino for two nights. They asked me for help because I've lived here for a long time and know a lot of people. I know a lot of people through various community organizations — and through the Chinese TV channel. I do not host the programs, but my husband is their permanent member and we take part in their special functions. My brother was one of the initiators of this Chinese TV station. It's great to have this channel for those who don't understand English....

I got involved in the *W5* protest for the sake of our children's future education. We put up notices in Chinatown about films explaining the incident, and some of these notices were torn down by people with bad intentions. Altogether there were only about a dozen to twenty people going to Edmonton for the big protest march. I even brought my son with me. It was very cold and he cried. I said, "Standing in the cold here is not for your mom or dad. We will never have the chance to study. We are doing this for *you*." He was about ten at the time. He sort of understood what I meant.

We have also canvassed for the Conservatives. Last time we helped John Turner. This time the PC candidate, I think he's good to the Chinese community. He doesn't particularly help the Chinese, but he keeps in touch with our community. He sends us Christmas cards and every time he comes here, we are invited to the banquet. And whenever any representatives from the Chinese government came here, we would take part in their activities. Whenever there are needs, we help out a bit. Sometimes we go to the Kee Ying building and talk to the elderly there, hoping that they can support the Conservative candidate.

WINNIE NG

Sometimes I get tired and down, but I get regenerated by my work in the community. You get a lot of energy back from going into a plant, meeting workers and teaching English in the workplace. It gives you the *why*. I was doing a health and safety workshop for Chinese auto workers. These were the people who were being used to clean up toxic spills without protective gear — without the proper training or knowledge of English. They didn't understand the hazards of the job — and they were only getting one extra hour of pay as a bonus. As a result, these Chinese workers had a lot of health problems. They were saying to me, "In the eighteenth century there was black slavery. Now in the twentieth century, it's yellow slavery." The impact of that statement stays in my mind... People might brand me as a socialist or whatever, but if there's going to be any division between classes, well you know which side I'd be on (laugh).

Looking back at the last ten years or so, I've moved gradually out of working within the Chinese Canadian community into working within the larger labour movement and women's movement, getting into political circles. But the more involved I get in these other areas, the more I realize that my roots are in the Chinese community. To people in other sectors, I will always be perceived as a Chinese Canadian woman. The label will always be there and it's very important that the issues and knowledge I get from other sectors be brought back to the Chinese community. No matter how much you involve yourself in other community work, you will still be recognized as a "Chinese Canadian woman".…. The further you move away from that base, the closer you get to it (laugh).

Eventually, what I'd love to see is an organization set up for the workers. You look around and see all these professional organizations and Lions Clubs for Chinese Canadians. But where are the labour organizations in that context? Some women have said, "Let's organize a women workers' organization." But working in ESL programs in industrial settings, I realize that men are also in bad shape to some extent. It's something we need to have more discussion about.

From what I've written, people know I've been very critical of the mainstream women's movement for not recognizing the important contributions and concerns of immigrant women and non-white women in this country. They can very well say that the organization is open — "come and participate." But, the reality is that the door has not been open — and you get tired of knocking on that door.

I see myself as a feminist in the sense that I am very sensitive to inequalities in the workplace. Feminism itself is a political statement that women need to be recognized as equal partners. Until issues like daycare, pay equity, employment equity, access to services and affordable housing are addressed adequately, I think these issues will remain broad political issues. I don't see how one can be a political and community activist without being a feminist. It's all encompassing and interrelated.

You need a certain level of humour and optimism (laugh) to go with your work. It's also being able to see the issues broader than the Canadian context — in a more global, international context — what the multinationals are doing in Hong Kong and the Philippines — the things that are going on in South Africa and Central America. You sort of make that connection with other workers. Eventually, I hope that workers here will see that connection somehow — and recognize that there needs to be international solidarity amongst workers.

I have a very clear political vision of what should be the ideal situation. Somehow all we're doing is working our way along. It's this vision of mine that keeps me going within the Chinese Canadian community and the larger Canadian community. This ideology and vision have been the "why" for my existence. I'm not going to be a martyr (laugh). I don't pretend to be one. You just take on whatever you can.

The whole concept of multiculturalism has been camouflaging the real issue, the inequality within the system — the institutionalized racism and discrimination that goes on. Instead of addressing the issues head on, they try to co-opt or appease the "ethnic" communities. There hasn't been enough political discussion about racism. Maybe people choose to ignore it because they don't want to rock the boat too much.

Around 1979 I started organizing for the boat people. We held our first meeting at my house. There was still debate about whether or not we should even take up the issue, since these boat people were actually middle class people.... Should we really be helping these "economic refugees"? Ultimately, we decided to support them on humanitarian grounds.

The Southeast Asian refugee issue got a lot of volunteers out. A lot of momentum was generated. Within a week, we got close to 10,000 signatures on petitions. Those volunteers and resources sort of continued when the W5 issue came along. It was a natural extension.

As a result of W5, the women's committee of the CCNC was set up. It was initiated by Angela Djao of Saskatoon at the first national meeting in Toronto. No one could possibly say no to the idea. But actions speak louder than words. They only gave the committee $500 as a budget, so nothing really happened.

The four years I worked at the Immigrant Women's Centre reaffirmed my politics. It gave me the opportunity to make connections with different immigrant groups. I saw a cross section of immigrants. I saw that the concerns and experiences were quite similar — the aspirations, frustrations — and pain. They were up against the same roadblocks. But we could only focus on health issues, while I felt a need to go beyond that.

In terms of my political involvement, I've always been a volunteer for Dan Heap. I also worked very hard to get John Sewell re-elected as mayor, so it was a big disappointment when he lost because of the police reform and gay community issues. When John Sewell announced his resignation as alderman, a couple of NDP people approached me and tried to talk me into running for the nomination. It came as such a surprise. It got me thinking about it. I felt it was important in the Chinese community that we not support a candidate simply on the basis of a shared heritage — first and foremost, we have to review the kinds of politics and issues that the person represents. We have too many issues where the Chinese Canadian politicians try to speak on behalf of the whole community. I thought that maybe it was time for the Chinese community to have someone who is Chinese Canadian, but with more progressive politics and grassroots experience as an alternative. I thought that the next generation could have a different kind of model as a politician, someone who could speak on behalf of women — on behalf of workers.

I decided to run three weeks before the nomination meeting. If I could get elected, I would put forward the whole issue of poverty as one theme to be addressed by the city. I thought that the poverty and human rights issue encompassed the health care and housing issues. This was 1984. It was very draining. I encountered a bit of discrimination, not because of my colour, but because of my platform. I'd call up people on the Toronto Islands and they'd say, "Poverty, human rights and racism? These aren't mainstream issues that concern us." In any case, I think we stunned and scared them (laugh). The race was so close. I lost by three or four votes. It was frustrating because both my parents and I could not vote because we lived on the west side, outside the ward (laugh).

Actually, losing the nomination was perhaps a mixed blessing. It was a relief not to have to be the person in front (laugh). Would I run again? I'll never say never.[4]

Notes

1. Mon Sheong Home for the Aged — Toronto's first home for Chinese senior citizens. It is located in the heart of Toronto's Chinatown.
2. A 1979 CTV news program portrayed Chinese Canadians as "foreigners" taking away places in universities from (white) Canadian students.
3. University Settlement House — an institution founded in 1910 to serve Toronto's immigrant community.
4. In 1992 Winnie Ng won the NDP nomination to run for MP for Toronto's Trinity-Spadina riding in the next federal election.

BIOGRAPHICAL NOTES

*As noted in our introduction, we could not publish the
stories of all the women who were interviewed. However, we
believe that the theme section of our book provides a pretty
fair sample of the 130 interviews we collected. The women
included in this section are listed below — along with a few
biographical details.*

CAROLINE CHAN was born in 1950 in the town of Truro, New
Brunswick. Later her family moved to Saint John, New Brunswick
and established a restaurant which Caroline helped to manage
when she graduated from university. At the time of her interview,
she was still residing in St. John.

VELMA CHAN was born in Merritt, B.C., in 1908. She helped run
the family grocery store for several years and also raised four
children. At the time of her interview, she was residing in Vancouver and learning Mandarin.

MAY CHEUNG was born in Guangdong, China, in 1935. She
immigrated to Canada in 1956, settling in Toronto. She has worked
for many years as a sewing machine operator. At the time of her
interview, she was still residing in Toronto.

MAY CHOW was born in Toisan, China, in 1937. She immigrated
to Canada in 1953, sponsored by her father who had come almost
twenty years before her. At the time of her interview, she was
residing in Kamloops, B.C.

IRENE CHU was born in Shanghai, China in 1938. She immigrated
to Canada in 1963 and did post-graduate work at McGill University before settling in Toronto. She taught for a while and then
decided to devote her time and energy to her family and fundrais-

ing for charities. She was a citizenship court judge from 1985 to 1986 and has been a member of the Canadian Immigration and Refugee Review Board, Appeal Division, since 1986.

ANNE FONG is a pseudonym for a woman who was born in Calgary in 1933. At the time of her interview, she was still residing there.

TAM GOOSEN was born in Hong Kong in 1947 and immigrated as a single woman to Canada in 1970. She has a masters degree in Chinese and Japanese History and is currently in her second term as a school trustee in the city of Toronto.

FERN HUM was born in Sudbury, Ontario, in 1950. She has been involved in Toronto's Chinese Canadian community as a board member of University Settlement House and as an advocate of the Heritage Language program. At the time of her interview, she was residing in Toronto.

GRACE LEE was born in Victoria, B.C., in 1902. She moved to China with her parents in 1911 and returned to Victoria by herself in 1928 to pursue a teaching career. She has devoted her entire life to teaching and learning. When interviewed, she was still residing in Victoria.

JEAN LEE was born in Windsor, Ontario, in 1919. As a child, she worked in the family restaurant. Since 1958 she and her husband have operated a successful store in Windsor, selling boats and marine supplies.

LIL LEE was born in Nanaimo, B.C., in 1927. She has raised four children here and is proud of the fact that they all want to go to China to study. When interviewed, she was living in Vancouver where she is active in the Chinese community.

DR. LINDA LEE was born in Toronto in 1953. She grew up in Toronto's Cabbagetown district and received her degree in dentistry from the University of Toronto. At the time of her interview, she was teaching dentistry in Saskatoon.

LINDA LEE was born in Halifax, Nova Scotia, in 1950. At the time of her interview, she was living in Halifax and working as a lawyer, specializing in corporate, commercial and real estate law.

MAE LEE was born in Union Bay, B.C., in 1915. She was one of the first Chinese Canadian women to work as a stockbroker. Mae was interviewed with her daughter, Sandra. At the time of the interview, she was residing in Vancouver.

SANDRA LEE was born in Victoria, B.C., in 1937. Like her mother, Mae, Sandra is a very independent and resourceful woman. She says that when her mother named her, she didn't want to want a little "Lotus Blossom," so she named her "Shui Hau," basically a boy's name. When interviewed, she was residing in Vancouver.

SHIN MEI LIN was born in Indonesia in 1936. She went to Taiwan at the age of eighteen and studied nursing. In 1965 she immigrated to Canada with her husband who was a doctor. They settled in Halifax where she continued her nursing career. When interviewed, she was still living in Halifax.

ROSE LUMB was born in Victoria, B.C., in 1928. She was the tenth child in a family of eleven children. She has been involved in various family businesses throughout her life while raising a family and volunteering in the community. In 1986 Rose received the Honourary Citizen of Victoria award.

MAY MAH was born in Hong Kong in 1933 and immigrated to Canada in 1953. She worked very hard for many years to support her entire family back home and help them to immigrate to Canada. At the time of her interview, she was residing in Calgary.

VALERIE MAH, a third generation Chinese Canadian, was born in Brockville, Ontario, in 1938. She currently resides in Toronto where she is an elementary school vice-principal. She is a prominent spokesperson in the Chinese Canadian community in Toronto and has served on the Ontario Advisory Council on Multiculturalism and various boards of directors.

RAMONA MAR was born in Fort Smith, Northwest Territories, in 1957. She has spent most of her life in Vancouver where she has worked in radio and television as a producer and writer. At present, she is living in Vancouver and taking time off to raise her son.

MARY MOHAMMED was born in Halifax, Nova Scotia, in 1931. She has lived in Winnipeg and Vancouver, but her home base is Halifax. She was residing there at the time of her interview.

WINNIE NG was born in Hong Kong in 1951. She came to Canada as a student in 1968 and decided to stay, settling in Toronto. Winnie got involved in the labour movement, becoming the first Chinese Canadian union organizer of women garment workers. She was also instrumental in establishing the Immigrant Women's Health Centre in Toronto. Currently, she is executive assistant to the Ontario Minister of Citizenship, and in May, 1992, she was nominated as the NDP candidate for the federal riding of Trinity-Spadina.

BETTY TOY was born in Windsor, Ontario, in 1956. She worked as a teacher in Brampton before returning to university to study commerce. She worked for an accounting firm in Toronto for a while, and then spent some time travelling. When interviewed, she was residing in Windsor.

LILY WELSH was born in China in 1950. She immigrated to Canada as an infant in 1951. She and her family settled in Unity, Saskatchewan. In 1968, she moved to Edmonton to go to university. At the time of her interview, she was working as an elementary school teacher in Edmonton.

SHIRLEY WELSH was born in China in 1949. She immigrated to Canada in 1954. She grew up in small towns in Saskatchewan where her family operated restaurants. At the time of her interview, Shirley was residing in Edmonton.

FRANCIS WONG was born in Brantford, Ontario, in 1921. She grew up in London, Ontario, with her good friend, Gretta (Wong) Grant. At the time of her interview, she was running a family drapery business in London.

MARY WONG was born in Hamilton, Ontario, in 1919. She worked very hard in her own restaurant business in Hamilton for more than forty years. She has also been actively involved in community work, describing herself as a "people person." Before retiring, she spent some years as a citizenship court judge.

MYRTLE WONG was born in Bendigo, Australia, in 1922. When she was growing up, her family moved back and forth between Australia and Hong Kong. In 1946 Myrtle came to Canada as a war bride, settling in London, Ontario. She was still living in London at the time of her interview.

SALLY WONG was born in Hong Kong in 1962. She immigrated to Canada in 1968. The family settled in the Riverdale area of East Toronto. At the time of her interview, she was residing in Edmonton, Alberta.

JANE WOO is a pseudonym for a woman who was born in Victoria, B.C., in 1928. At the time of her interview, she was residing in Winnipeg.

VICTORIA YIP was born in Victoria in 1911. She lost her mother at a young age and was raised by a very sensitive and non-sexist father. At the time of her interview, she was residing in Vancouver and keeping very busy, learning new things and meeting new people. She describes herself as a "liberated woman long ago."

KEEP LISTENING

After the completion of a first draft of this book, the editorial committee got together for an informal, round table, wrap-up session. The discussion which took place was a very worthwhile and necessary process for all of us. We learned a lot from each other. As an epilogue to this book, we decided to share excerpts from that wrap-up session...

JULIA: Winnie, you originally wanted a booklet, and now...

WINNIE: It was so long ago (laugh). I can't remember anymore....

I think back in '85, we were looking for curriculum materials for ESL workplace programs. I was using these Portuguese women's life stories in Canada. That sort of triggered off the idea of developing our own materials on Chinese Canadian women. We kept our eyes open for any books or articles on Chinese Canadians. Basically, we couldn't find anything that reflected the voices of Chinese Canadian women.... So we started this project. We were thinking of a booklet with photos and simple stories in plain English for immigrant Chinese women. The goal was to use their oral histories as a document — to give them the recognition for their contribution to the community.... When we started, it wasn't as ambitious as what we have now. The ideas got expanded. It grew into a national project — from a booklet to this book.

JULIA: And I think the women's committee of the CCNC knew that something was lacking. There were so few of us. We were hoping that this project could draw on experiences from Chinese women across the country, through the local chapters — with the aim of establishing a Chinese Canadian women's network in the future....

A few local committees started — like in London, Vancouver, Edmonton and Montreal. But we've still got a long way to go in forming a strong Chinese Canadian women's network.

DORA: There's a lot of sexism in the community and in the board, but the men refuse to recognize it. The issue was raised at the Edmonton CCNC National Conference in '83, and there was total denial.

JULIA: There was only one woman delegate present at the CCNC national conference in Windsor. So in 1986 we asked all the local chapters to send at least one female representative.

AMY: We spent an hour talking about women's issues at the presidents' meeting in Ottawa in 1990 — still a lot of denial from the men. Many were questioning the need to even discuss women's issues. The attitude was "What are women's issues, anyway?"

WINNIE: I don't think it got that much attention from the men. Basically, they see it as a fundraising project. You know, keep the women happy with their own little project, but don't start setting up a separate organization....

DORA: And don't draw the resources away from the main CCNC issues.

JULIA: I don't think this is an isolated case. You see a lot of organizations within the Chinese Canadian community dominated by men — organizations in which women do a lot of work that goes unrecognized.

MAY: Isn't it true that it's mostly women who do the actual leg work, organizing and community work, right? While the men end up being the leaders, the spokespersons.

DORA: Most of what has been written about our community is from a white, male perspective. I think this book allows the community to speak on its own behalf. We have a very rich, involved history. A lot of people don't understand it because they simply don't know about it. So this book is very valuable, particularly for Canadian-born Chinese. It's a first step.

AMY: It's a small piece in conjunction with a lot of other things we're doing — like the Chinese Exclusion and Head Tax Redress campaign. Honestly, I don't think this book will reach all Chinese Canadian women out there. The women who don't speak English — I don't think they'd even know about the book unless we translated it. We should try and translate it.

MAY: But this book — in English — would reach children. That's the group it's targeting. The book would be important to Chinese Canadians growing up here because when you're growing up here, there are no books that speak about your own experience. All the books are about white Canadians. It's a feeling that you have no place here. You're not even represented in Canadian literature.

DORA: The book is there. It can be accessed by basically anyone. It's just a matter of your time.

AMY: For the women out there, their concerns are day to day — to survive. Economically, they are not in a good position in the current recession. Buying a book is probably the last thing they'll ever think of doing — even if it's about Chinese Canadian women. What I'm saying is that this book is a step forward, but we should view it in conjunction with so many other actions that need to be taking place — to make real changes in people's lives.

TERRY: I think the point is well taken, May, that the book serves a significant role in making us visible for the younger generation. For me, it seems that not all ethnic groups in Canada are equally invisible, or as badly represented as we are. At this point, the Chinese community should be able to tap financial resources within the community to make us more visible. My question is why haven't we produced more material since we have the financial resources to do so? I really don't understand it.

JULIA: Well, I think the community is still struggling for survival. It's not just a matter of more money to produce more books. There's still a lot of sexism within the community. Chinese women are still oppressed — simply not recognized as important. The image of a woman as a submissive, dependent object in the family is still very pervasive. I think this book will be very educational for our community, as well as for any other community. Certainly it will encourage more of a linkage between Chinese Canadian women and other women's groups.

TERRY: For me, there's a whole range of issues or problems. Julia is saying that there's still sexism in the community. Yes, but then, how is it different from the mainstream sexism? The thing is we're not a homogenous community. In terms of class differences and cultural differences, there are some diverse groups within the Chinese community — groups from different parts of China, from Taiwan, from Hong Kong, from other parts of Southeast Asia — and then Canadian-born.... In the book, we even have a woman from Australia. Also who are we as a community — what are our cultural roots? How do we recover a tradition which is heavily misogynist — in terms of the last eight hundred years, footbinding and so on. Where do we want to go? What are the good things within the Chinese tradition?.... A lot of questions in my mind are not answered.

WINNIE: I think the book got a bit away from the original intent of being a whole lot more accessible to the immigrant women workers. However, I can see it reaching out to a broader audience. I see the book as more of a means, rather than an end. It should spark a whole lot of creative, follow-up projects — music, novels, film, theatre. The key point, depending on how we do our promotion, is to make sure all the educational institutions across the country have copies. We've collected a wealth of material, but we've just scratched the surface.

MAY: We have to admit that this book is not representative of all Chinese Canadian women. There were not enough working class women interviewed. And we never interviewed any lesbian women about what it means to deal with issues of sexuality in our community. These are important points to keep in mind for further projects like this.

DORA: Like anything, when you finish reading this book, you look back and say, "Well, we could've done this — we could've done that." But in comparison with what's out there, it's the best thing that we do have.

JULIA: I think we have to be very positive about this project. Looking at the whole experience, I think we also grew with this book, too. You know, working together, struggling with how to produce it. Learning from each other.... Personally, I think I gained a lot — although it's been a *long* process. If we ever do a second volume, we'll do better, much better. And I think we could share our experience with other women's groups doing similar projects.

WINNIE: On a personal level, just reading it, it's quite a learning experience in itself — how rich, how *simple*, how hard it is too — all at the same time. It's quite a humbling experience — the strength in these stories.

DORA: We've also created a very valuable resource — not just in terms of this completed book, but also with all the other interviews and photographs that didn't get included. So at least in Toronto, we have probably one of the most extensive collections on Chinese Canadian history — from the community, not written by someone else or based on government documents.

AMY: I came in without expecting anything in particular. So when I first read the initial manuscript, I was really *impressed and inspired* by ... how tough these women were.

WINNIE: What surprised me was how similar all the stories are in a way, that underlying ... strength ... you know, hardship and how simple their lives were. They carry on their daily living — it's a task. So that's where I felt, well, it's no different for women whether they are from China or anywhere, who are struggling to make a living.

TERRY: That's certainly true. Also, I think in terms of the old stereotype of Chinese women being submissive and passive — you know, it's like this book put that stereotype to rest. (Laughter)

JULIA: What surprised me was how important their contribution was to the growth of the Chinese community. All the different works they've done — with the children, the schools, volunteer work in the community. They've accomplished a lot. But their work hasn't really been recognized.

TERRY: That's my problem with any literature available now on Chinese women. A lot of it is actually written by Westerners. There's this underlying message, "Well, these women have been oppressed for thousands and thousands of years...." You get a sense that they're just little worms. It really makes me angry. You know from your own experience that this is a false image of Chinese women, but you don't have any literature to back you up. I think this book, although it's not perfect, really goes a long way to dispel that stereotype.

MAY: Yes, when you read these stories of other women, you read about yourself in a way too. I think of the word "recognition." You know, "That's my mother." "That's my grandmother."

DORA: Unlike most other immigrant groups, there was legislation that these women had to deal with — legislation that largely shaped the direction of their lives. In spite of it, they were determined to create as normal a lifestyle for themselves and their children as was possible at that time.

MAY: It was amazing. They were creating it out of such isolation. Under those conditions of isolation, these women managed to raise families, build vibrant communities and remain very strong.

DORA: I've talked to older second and third generation Chinese Canadians about their apparent acceptance of their circumstances — even in light of the Head Tax redress campaign now, why so many of the war veterans aren't speaking up. Their position has been, "Look, as each day goes by, things look better than they looked yesterday." I spoke to one woman who was finally hired as a secretary and she made it known that she was hired by a Jewish company because they know what it's like to be discriminated against — and she thought she was *really, really* lucky to be hired. So there's this don't rock the boat attitude. We are grateful that we're making progress.

Somebody else down the road can be the one to be the shit disturber. We have to pay the rent. We've got kids who go to school.... It's a survival tactic.

TERRY: I'd say in a very general way that maybe that has something to do with the culture, you know, that acceptance and the whole sense of continuity. We won't fight for it now, but our children will or our grandchildren will....

DORA: We didn't interview as many women as we could who were involved in the war effort. We interviewed a couple in Victoria and there was absolutely no sign of being passive there. The women were very aggressive in their fundraising. They raised enough money to buy an ambulance for China. The Chinese community doesn't have a history of being passive about asserting their rights. I mean, they were signing petitions to the Canadian government in the 1850s and 1860s....

MAY: I think we saw a lot of women fighters in this book. I mean, there's a certain amount of *acceptance* among the women, but a lot of times acceptance is a *strength*, right? You accept what you have to accept — and that's certainly not the easiest thing to do. These women had to accept the political, economic and social conditions under which they lived. But at the same time they were fighting it in different ways, often in small ways. They were holding their families together and building communities.

DORA: A lot of it has to do with the fact that historians haven't had access to Chinese Canadian resources. They don't have the language facilities. I think Chinese Canadian history is a very new area.

My position is very strong that it's not simply a matter of being born here as a Canadian. The experiences of aunts, uncles, grandparents were passed on to us as well. That's why we really need to know what happened when *they* were growing up. Yes, there were a lot of negative experiences there, but again, in spite of all the negative elements, you see a very small, relatively cohesive and vibrant community emerging during the thirties and forties. The attitudes, the lack of opportunities, what they were doing at the time — the Chinese community then was so different from what we see today. Yet you talk to these people now in their seventies and eighties — are they hostile? No, there's a strange absence of resentment.

WINNIE: Maybe that was something we didn't probe into when we were doing interviews for the book. Where do these women draw their strength and support from? In the video *Black Mother, Black Daughter* (NFB film by Sylvia Hamilton), you see older black women in Nova Scotia who had come up from the States to escape slavery.... The church was quite prominent as a source of strength for these women. They also drew strength from each other, from that community network. And maybe that's a part that's missing from our stories.

DORA: The church was very important to the Chinese community in Toronto. At one time seventy percent of the community were Christians. So when the Chinese came here from Vancouver, the missionaries took them in and gave them English classes. They saw their friends there. Parents and children got involved in church organizations. You had a social network through the church — at least for the community in Ontario.

MAY: In terms of where the Chinese community in Canada is going, this book doesn't really continue on to how the community changed after the sixties when they finally opened the doors to a lot more immigration, right? We've got all these very different communities within the Chinese community. I mean, it's a good question — how the older communities can work with the new communities.

TERRY: That's still another book. (Laughter)

MAY: Yeah, it's another book. There are a lot of hard questions that we can't find the answers for yet.... There are a lot of divisions that can be used to divide the community. But at the same time, racism kind of lumps us together. So we have to really think hard about getting organized within the community — when we have diverse languages, diverse classes, diverse histories and cultures.

AMY: I don't see a strong, unanimous voice in any community — or a consensus on any position — even on racism, national unity, environmental issues! Why should we expect the Chinese community to be any different from any other communities in that respect? But of course, from our perspective as Chinese Canadians we are fighting racism, but who wants to get the message out, so it's not such a lonely battle? It seems that only a few people are involved, you know.

WINNIE: But I think one of the things that needs to be straightened out too, is that we as Chinese Canadians have always been there fighting against racism.

DORA: I think a lot depends on whether or not the larger community is prepared to listen.

JULIA: It seems that fighting racism and sexism is seen as the responsibility of the visible minorities or women. I think these should be issues for *all* Canadians to address — not just issues of Chinese Canadians or Canadian women.

DORA: The Chinese community has been speaking out against the way we've been treated for several decades. There's documentation on that.

AMY: That's what I'm saying — this *perceived* silence is playing to the advantage of the dominant cultural group. They always want to play up this image.

DORA: Yeah, one of the arguments at the turn of the century was that, "You're a sojourner — you don't plan to stay...you've always planned to go back." But what makes us any different than the Italians or the Irish who always say, "When I go home, when I go home..." But they don't end up going home.

TERRY: Perhaps my choice is not to fight on a public level, but on a private, individual level. And I'm very resentful of the fact that it is not recognized. I don't particularly want to be public about my opinions. Our community is not homogenous. We're different from each other in many ways. So let us be different. There are different ways of fighting. When you do go public, you only have Chinese fighting for the Chinese, the Blacks fighting for the Blacks.

When you're being discriminated against, you fight for your own group — then they can use that and turn it around and say that you only fight for your own group.... I think what Julia is saying is very well-taken. It's a Canadian issue — not a minority issue — not a white versus colour issue.

WINNIE: Sure, there are different ways of fighting, but I think that one of the key points is to make the fight public too. There are different people in the community taking on different roles. But I still feel you need that *concerted* effort to make sure that the message gets across. And that it's not just one community for its own community. It's making links, building up the coalitions — like in the women's movement.

MAY: And that's crucial — now more than ever. I'd like to see us organizing and working with other communities experiencing the same kinds of problems — like the native communities who have survived and withstood five hundred years of attempted genocide and injustice on this continent. There's a real need now, more than ever, to make our voices heard — to get together and reclaim our histories. *Jin Guo: Voices of Chinese Canadian Women* is a first step. So keep listening....

GLOSSARY

Reference to Chinese terms are either in Cantonese, the dialect spoken in the area near Canton city (Guangzhou) in Guangdong province, or Toisanese, a dialect of Cantonese, spoken in *Sai Yip*, the "Four Counties," not far from Canton city in the Pearl River Delta. Most of the early immigrants from China to North America came from this area.

bak	term of respect used to address an older man. Literally means "elder uncle" (Cantonese/Toisanese)
bok choy	Chinese greens (Toisanese)
cha siu	barbecued pork (Cantonese)
Ching Ming	Each year families will go to the cemetery to pay their respects to their ancestors and to repair the headstones and plant flowers. (Cantonese)
goy (Cantonese)	to change (*gai* — Mandarin)
guat hau	to shave the head (Toisanese); *muan yet* — the celebration of the first month of birth. Babies traditionally receive their first hair cuts (*guat hau*) on this day. (Toisanese)
gui lo	literally "old ghost," pejorative term used to refer to non-Chinese, usually of European descent. (Cantonese)
gum san	"Gold Mountain," the name Chinese used in referring to North America. First used to describe San Francisco. British Columbia became Canada's *gum san*.
heung ha	one's home village. (Cantonese/Toisanese)
hoo sang	local born or Canadian-born. (Toisanese)
to sang	local or Canadian-born (Cantonese)
hsien seng	means "Mr." or "teacher." When used by

women, usually means her husband. (Cantonese \ Toisanese)

joss stick fragrant tinder mixed with clay and used as incense.

juk sing pejorative term used to refer to Chinese born in Canada. It literally means a stick of bamboo which is naturally hollow, cut off at both ends — meaning that those Chinese born in Canada are not really Chinese, but not entirely Canadian either. (Cantonese/ Toisanese)

Kuan yin Buddhist deity, often referred to as the goddess of mercy and peace. (Cantonese)

lo fan literally "old foreigner," term used to refer to non-Chinese persons of European ancestry. (Cantonese/Toisanese)

mah jong Chinese game involving four people and played with tiles. (Cantonese)

mui tsai literally means "little sister"— a euphemism for a girl from a poor family who was sold to another family to serve as a domestic servant. (See Introduction.) (Cantonese)

suk literally means father's younger brother, but is also used as a form of address to a man who is about one's father's age. (Cantonese /Toisanese)

tai Chinese pastries

tong association, as in family association or clan. (Cantonese)